THE ART OF
Wild SWIMMING
ENGLAND & WALES

Everything you need to know
and over 100 amazing locations

**ANNA DEACON &
VICKY ALLAN**

BLACK & WHITE PUBLISHING

First published 2021
by Black & White Publishing Ltd
Nautical House, 104 Commercial Street, Edinburgh, EH6 6NF

1 3 5 7 9 10 8 6 4 2   21 22 23 24

ISBN: 978 1 78530 359 3

Text copyright © Vicky Allan and Anna Deacon 2021

All photography except images listed on page 248 © Anna Deacon 2021

The right of Anna Deacon and Vicky Allan to be identified as the authors and photographer of this work has been asserted by them in accordance with the Copyright, Designs and Patents Act 1988.

All rights reserved.
No part of this publication may be reproduced, stored in a retrieval system, or transmitted in any form, or by any means, electronic, mechanical, photocopying, recording or otherwise, without permission in writing from the publisher.

This book is based in part on interviews about the lives and experiences of its contributors. In some cases names have been changed solely to protect the privacy of others. The authors have stated to the publishers that the contents of these interviews are true and accurate to the best of their knowledge.

The Art of Wild Swimming isn't a guide to swimming safety and therefore neither the authors nor the publisher can accept any responsibility for damage of any kind, to property or persons, that occurs either directly or indirectly from the use of this book or from any wild swimming activity.

A CIP catalogue record for this book is available from the British Library.

Layout by Black & White Publishing
Printed and bound in Croatia by Grafički Zavod Hrvatske

To our swim clans,
with love

───────────────

Rob, Lily and Finlay

Andy, Louis and Max

River Thames

CONTENTS

**THE ART OF
THE PLUNGE**   1
A hive mind in your kitbag
The maps inside our heads

21 reasons to swim   13

**FLOAT LIKE
A STARFISH**   21
The safe dipping code
Be drowning aware
Locating your swim

**BODIES OF
WATER**   27
The sea · Reservoirs · Lakes · Waterfalls ·
Rivers · Crackers about ice

**HOW TO BE AN
AWESOME WILD
SWIMMER**   61
Codes of conduct
Gilly McArthur's guide to biosecurity
Access which areas?
Where the wild things are
Wildlife at heart
Aqua activism

THE BIG CHILL   75
Three things about cold
Wild swimming with kids
Stoking the fire inside
Shivery bites & hot flasks

SKINS OR SUITS?   85
What's in your kitbag?

**OH, THE PLACES
YOU'LL GO!**   89
In England

**OH, THE PLACES
YOU'LL GO!**   197
In Wales

SEA'S THE DAY   227
21 challenges to make you extra
  swim happy
Finding your own paradise

This map is for you to draw	243
Locations, locations, locations	244
Books you might enjoy	247
Image credits	248
Thank you	249
About the authors	250

Blea Tarn

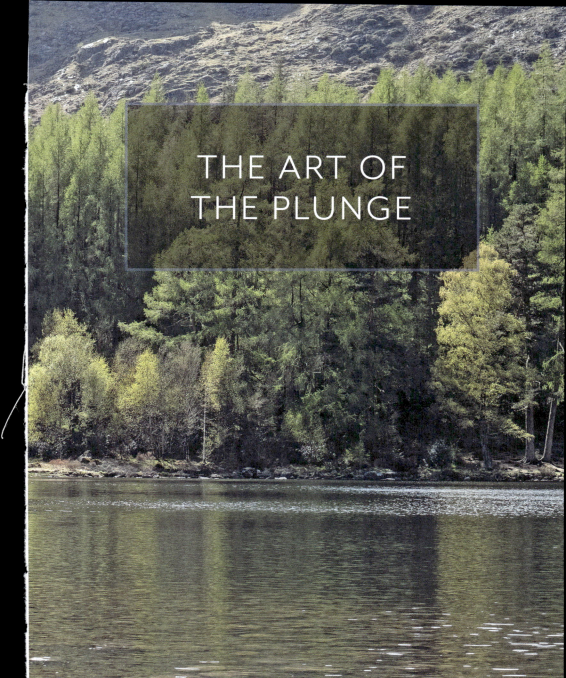

THE ART OF THE PLUNGE

A HIVE MIND IN YOUR KITBAG

Imagine, we thought, a book that would be a map, not just to the places to swim – the waterways, lakes and beaches – but to those who swim there. Imagine that book were a guide to how to be the best, safest, most responsible and joyous swimmer you can be. Imagine it in your kitbag.

That was the idea behind this book. It would be like your own personal swim coach and guide, there for you wherever you swim.

And we wanted the map not just to be our map, but the map of many, a community, and the starting point for those who read it to create their own maps, their own art of swimming. It would be your map too.

We felt that everything we knew about wild swimming had come from someone else who knew a lot more about it or about how to swim in a particular place or type of water. Some of that had come from people Anna and I had met, when we wrote our first book, *Taking the Plunge*, some from swimmers we had met since, some from the hive mind of the wild swimming community. These were our teachers in this particular art.

We thought if we could put all that in a book – all those wonderful, smart and quirky tips – then that would be the book we might want in our own kitbag. Water-stained, scribbled over, but hopefully never entirely drenched.

And that this guide would be a book like the voice of all the people who had ever told us something smart or funny or vital about·why, how or where to swim. Because one voice is not enough.

But at the same time, we were keen that this book – the imaginary one in our kitbags – would not only tell us vital information about how to keep safe or where to find the best post-dook café, but also push us to do all the right things in terms of looking after the waters we so love.

What quickly became clear, when we got in touch with our wild swimming friends and heroes is that most of them did want to share what they do and how they do it. But they were keen to pick places that weren't sitting on fragile ecosystems or hadn't already been made vulnerable by the impact of other travellers.

They were also often concerned about how we encourage people to wild swim in a country where many bodies of water, or entries to them, are only accessible through trespass. Access, in England and

Wales, is often a limiting factor on where we can swim, but there are many campaigns, which you can get involved in, which seek to push for greater access.

One of the big challenges for all of us is to do what we love, and even spread our love of it, while ensuring that the waters and ecosystems that offer us such joy remain undamaged. So when we decided to write a guide we were presented with a challenge. How do we encourage people, while making sure that we're not sending a horde of humans out into nature to make a big messy footprint?

As swimmers, we feel we need to be nature's ambassadors, cleaning and caring for our environment wherever we go. We've found outdoor swimmers, for the most part, to be incredibly caring towards their swim spots. They often talk about leaving only footprints behind, taking only photographs, picking up litter others have left, improving on how things are found. But, across the UK, there is a major problem with our beautiful places being trashed by a few – from litter dropping to the lighting of fires to dangerous parking or thoughtless noise.

Over recent years, we've heard many people's swim stories and one of the things that strikes me is how often they will centre on place. They're not about some anonymous bit of water, but are descriptions of ventures into water of a particular loch, river, reservoir or bay. They are expressions of love. When we submerge in these aquatic worlds, we become attached.

All of us have our own swim journeys – our stories about what brought us to the water and made us want to keep coming back. When Anna and I started swimming this was the thing that fascinated us – the big question about *why* people swim. It's what set us off on our voyage of laughter, joy, curiosity and adventure, across country and community. It was at the heart of *Taking the Plunge*.

This book isn't just a guide, it's testimony to the love of swimmers for their local swim spots. Our contributors write passionately about the wildlife, the landscape, the nature of the water, its tides, currents, stillness, silkiness, roughness. It's a guide not just to geographic places, but our human connection with them.

THE MAPS INSIDE OUR HEADS

VICKY ALLAN,
Leith, Edinburgh
Journalist & author
ALLAN-VICKY

Now and again I'm asked when I became a wild swimmer, and mostly I say that I only really adopted the term about three years ago, when I began to develop a regular dipping routine in my local waters around Edinburgh as well as searching, outside town, for new places for a swim. Since people described this thing I was doing as wild swimming, I began calling it that too.

But really, the journey started long before that. It began when I was a teenager growing up in Northumberland and, with some friends, developed a habit of throwing myself into whatever body of cold water we came across. It was something we did. Anywhere, no matter how cold. Snow on the ground? Why not?

I was reminded of that on returning to Northumberland recently to walk St Cuthbert's Way. I wasn't born a wild swimmer on the beaches of Edinburgh; that happened in the seas and waterfall pools of the North East of England. The waterfall pool at Roughtin Linn. Cocklawburn Beach in the chill winter. The town beach at Spittal on the south side of Berwick-upon-Tweed.

This book is partly a guide as to where to go and how to swim – but it also documents the connection to place. Each entry is a love story to a particular location and the times spent in it; what it has given the humans who swam there.

We all have our own love stories. We have our maps too, like charts of old lovers, each in a different port, or maybe beach or quarry pool. Mine would feature the far beaches of Lindisfarne, the seaside towns of Whitley Bay, Scarborough: holidays from my childhood. I have a soft spot for the Cornish coast, where an ex-boyfriend's family, keen surfers and sailors, would frequently holiday. Their cousin Mary, in her eighties then, would swim daily in the sea

Hethpool Linn

off Penzance. Cousin Mary, I would often think, was the old woman I wanted to be.

But back in 2018 I can remember thinking that, there I was in my forties and I was far from on track to becoming that older woman. I began to wonder what it was that was holding me back. A friend who had lost her mum persuaded me to start taking a regular dip and it reminded me of how, a few years previously, in the summer following my brother's sudden death from a pulmonary embolism, the only place I had found solace was bobbing on my back in an Irish lough.

Around this time something happened that was life-altering. I met the inspiring Anna Deacon and started to swim with her. Before we knew it we had hatched a plan for a book and were travelling across Scotland to meet fellow swimmers.

That was the beginning of a connection to a swimming community, but also a new geography.

One of the pleasures of creating this book is the way it has expanded those maps in my head. When I think about the place I live in these days, it's often in terms of where it sits in relation to the sea. A map in my head is marked by three points of a triangle. Point one, my home. Point two, to the east, less than a fifteen-minute jog away, my nearest patch of sea. Then, point three, Wardie, the increasingly popular town beach which is reachable by a very pleasant but wandering cycle route.

It feels as if, when I think about it, my mind can reach out and take an imaginary dip.

But also, in writing this book, my mind has stretched out beyond those beaches, down the coast, to the Northumberland of my childhood, the London I lived in as an adult, to memories of lying down and sleeping in the grass after a delicious swim at Hampstead Ponds, to a dip at Grantchester Meadows, a twilight paddle at Margate, the white sand beaches of the Scilly Isles, Criccieth, Harlech Castle, tarns in the Lakes, the tidal mystery of Robin Hood's Bay.

More than that – it now reaches out to places as yet unvisited, as I've heard and read the tributes of others, and found myself desperate to go to their recommended places, to plunge in. And beyond that too, to places that are only an idea in my mind, that I might discover myself, because above all that's what we want to encourage. We want you to draw your own map.

Coves Haven, Lindisfarne
📍 **caskets.blissful.recover**

When the tide is out, the island's village can be busy with tourists, frenetic and a little overwhelming. But take a walk to the north of the isle, cross the expanse of dunes and you're in another world. There was no one on the beach when I arrived recently, only the fulmars watching from their cliff nook perches. The skerries of rock formed a perfect channel in which to have a gentle swim. Be careful, though, as you walk the dunes, not to pick up on your clothes any of the invasive piri piri burrs. And remember to keep an eye on the tide times if you're crossing back to the mainland: one of the tricky things about this swim is timing a dip with a high enough tide not to require a long wade, with the necessity of getting off the island in time. But that's the magic of Lindisfarne. It is a place of washings in and out, of water and tourists, in which the tide's comings and goings are never not felt.

Hethpool Linn, Northumberland
 rainfall.spouting.manhole

A waterfall, rich with dark peaty waters that have run down from the Cheviots and the College Valley. I came across it one day while walking, and tired and hot decided, since I had not packed my swimmers and no one was around apart from my walking friend, to take a dip. There's a perfect deep pool, just a short walk from the bridge, access on the right-hand side as you face eastwards (i.e. downstream), with only a small scramble down the hill to access it. Swim right up to its churning white water and feel like you're in an endless water mill. Look out for the feral goats, who may be watching. Park at the College Valley car park.

Hayburn Wyke, Yorkshire
 change.burglars.robes

Not exactly a swim, more of a delightful shower. There was something about the way this pretty little waterfall tumbled down into a pool on the beach that made it too tempting not to stop and wash down in the waters, on a walk along the coastal path, the Cleveland Way, between Robin Hood's Bay and Scarborough. The Hayburn Beck trickles or gushes down onto the shore, with a power depending on the recent rainfall, sometimes in one channel, sometimes two. The perfect pool in which to bathe and paddle, while looking out at the majestic seascape. Just don't expect not to have an audience: this stunning coastal path is, unsurprisingly, popular.

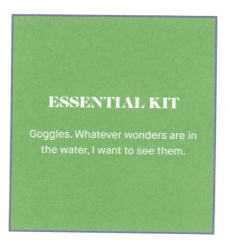

ESSENTIAL KIT

Goggles. Whatever wonders are in the water, I want to see them.

ANNA DEACON,
Edinburgh
Photographer & writer
WILDSWIMMINGSTORIES

Some of my happiest childhood memories centre around family walks which often led us to lakes, rivers and streams in which we played, swam and pottered about, as we had picnics or sausages over a fire, so I have always felt a real draw to be near the water.

When I was a child, we lived for a time in the Cotswolds and spent wonderful hazy summer days swimming in the manmade gravel pits. I remember lying on my back in the water and watching the bright blue dragonflies flitting about on the surface and feeling like it was pretty close to paradise. Then there was a sense of jeopardy after we found a huge dead pike on the shore near where we swam one day, the teeth on the aquatic beast quite put me off for some time!

I've enjoyed some beautiful swims in Hampstead Ponds – nestled in London's green heart the ponds feel like a precious secret in the winter, the mist on the surface, swimming eye to eye with the ducks, the slippery descent down the ladder into the cold. It seems so far removed from the rest of London, like you have been transported into some wild place.

The Lake District is somewhere I have enjoyed exploring more recently, connecting with some of the amazing wild swimming community who live there. This is just the most wonderful place to explore. What a paradise for swimmers, with waterfalls, lakes, tarns and rivers galore. My happiest days usually involve a hike to a new swim spot, an adventure with a friend, seeing what we can discover.

I love how the country changes so much as you travel around, from hills and dales to city swim spots, from expanses of wild sand dunes to winding rivers, from epic waterfalls to tiny coves and tidal pools. There is somewhere for everyone to explore. Water is everywhere.

I'm aware, though, of how in England and Wales the laws around access limit the places we can explore. Whereas in Scotland, key to our right to roam is the right to swim in any body of water. This is part of the debate we've chosen to highlight in this book and an issue of which we would like to raise the profile.

What I love most of all are the swimmers. Those people we have met in person, or simply connected with online, have inspired me so much to explore England and Wales more, to seek out adventures across the UK, to swim in tarns, rivers, reservoirs, lakes and the sea with these wonderful humans and to experience their favourite bodies of water.

Cotswolds Country Park & Lake
◉ **fuzzy.profiled.otters**

This is the gravel pit where I spent a lot of time as a child: it has definitely changed since then, but the essence of the place remains. It's the largest inland paddling beach in the UK, and so there is plenty of space to spread out. There are great facilities, including BBQ spots you can book. It is definitely more of a fun family day out than a peaceful secret swimming spot, but as I often have kids in tow when I swim I find this super handy. Be sure to book ahead on warm days and in the summer season (prices are as low as £1.80 for access).

Lake Windermere
◉ **exactly.holly.trickled**

I recently discovered Lake Windermere is easily accessed via public transport. It is a fabulous option if you don't have (or don't want to use) a car and are craving a beautiful swim. My trip involved a train from Edinburgh to Oxenholme, from where I jumped on a quick train direct to Windermere. The largest natural lake in England, Windermere is very popular with boats, so being seen is vital, as is knowing where to get in and swim safely. Please do be careful when the lake is busy. Miller Ground is a good spot to start from, a short walk from Windermere, and parking nearby takes you to the side of the lake, where you can wade in from the shallows or jump off the jetties. Soak up those wonderful views across the water!

Hampstead Ponds
◉ **front.froze.unique (mixed pond)**
◉ **punch.grit.stay (men's)**
◉ **sunk.crazy.weedy (women's)**

When I visit London I try and squeeze in a swim in this enchanting spot. It varies hugely from season to season, and if you're after a quiet swim then avoid sunny days in peak season. It's best enjoyed in the depths of winter or early morning before the crowds descend. Like a little pocket of magic hiding behind the trees, you honestly wouldn't know it's there.

This serene watery moment is abundant with wildlife and space too. The women's and men's ponds are open all year, but the mixed pond is closed in winter. All are lifeguarded and you must purchase a ticket, the cost of which is similar to a swim in a local sports centre. There are changing facilities and showers, and the ponds are easily accessible via public transport, by foot and bike.

Hampstead Ponds

21 REASONS TO SWIM

Not that we think you need persuading but, just in case you're feeling reluctant to dip a toe in the water, we couldn't resist listing a few of the many reasons to get wild swimming.

1 It's **exhilarating**, often giddy, silly and wildly playful. Need we say more?

2 It has all those health **benefits** that come with any form of exercise – swimming, whether indoors or outdoors, raises your heart rate, while taking impact stress off your body and improving muscle strength and cardiovascular fitness.

3 **Cold water shock** can be dangerous, but regular exposure to it can bring positives. It is a form of stress that exercises your body's reaction to stress, triggering our fight or flight response through what's called the sympathetic nervous system. That's why you feel all that panic and confusion when the icy cold first hits. Dr Mark Harper, a consultant anaesthetist who has researched cold water physiology, explained to us in *Taking the Plunge* that our bodies, these days, mostly experience low-level chronic stress, rather than intermittent big stress:

'We used to be worried,' he said, 'about running from sabre-toothed tigers, now it's running to get to a train on time. That low-level stress can be reduced. You can do it by adapting to cold water, which means you then cross-adapt to other stress.'

4 Dook your head under – or simply just your face, so you can keep your bobbly hat on! – and you stimulate another part of your nervous system, resulting in mental and physical health benefits. What's called the **dive reflex**, the splash of cold water on your face, stimulates your vagus nerve, activating your parasympathetic nervous system, slowing your heart, and putting your body into what's called rest and digest mode.

Mark Harper says, 'When you put your face in cold water, you get this massive parasympathetic stimulation and that reduces inflammation, and that works through the vagal nerve.' In effect, when you swim, you are exercising both these elements of your unconscious nervous system.

5 It gives you a biochemical **happiness fix** by triggering the release of endorphins. Of course, you can achieve this from going on a run or swimming indoors, but the great thing is that cold water swimming brings the endorphins on quicker, even in a brief dip.

6 Most swimmers testify to swimming having improved their **mental health**. Research into this is still in its early days, but a 2018 case report showed that a 24-year-old woman with symptoms of severe depression and anxiety who did a weekly programme involving cold water swimming found an improvement in mood after each swim and a sustained and gradual reduction in the symptoms of depression. After one year of therapy with cold water swimming, she was medication-free. A more recent small-scale trial conducted by Dr Mark Harper found 'significant reductions in the severity of depression and anxiety' following a course of outdoor swimming sessions.

7 You boost your **immune system**. Research on this is in its infancy, but it has been shown that cold water swimming boosts the number of white blood cells – an element of the immune system that helps your body fight off infection – circulating in a person's blood.

8 When done with others it's **enormously social**. There are parts of the swim community that are as much about getting together with other people and doing something daft or adventurous – about the cake and hot chocolate afterwards, the chat while bobbing in the ocean wearing a handknitted bobble hat – as getting the strokes in.

Many studies now show that exercising in a social group is better for us, in general, than lone exercise. One, published in *The Journal of the American Osteopathic Association* in 2017, found that those working out in a group experience more improvements in lowered stress and quality of life than those working out individually.

9 It may help **stave off dementia**. Research by scientists at the University of Cambridge found that long-term cold water swimmers had raised levels of the cold-shock protein called RBM3. In trials using mice, it has been found to possibly slow the onset of dementia. But lead scientist, Professor Giovanna Mallucci, did not recommend cold water plunges as an anti-dementia therapy, rather he indicated that they could point the way to new drug treatments.

10 It may help **prevent and reduce** those conditions characterised by high levels of inflammation, many of which are the key health problems of our times – diabetes, Alzheimer's, inflammatory bowel disease, fibromyalgia, even heart disease.

As Dr Mark Harper told us, 'Cold water swimming appears to be one way of dealing with inflammation, which itself is at the root of a lot of health problems.'

A key mechanism via which it does this is the dive reflex, which stimulates the parasympathetic nervous system to send out chemical messengers that lower heart rate and reduce inflammation, and also others that turn on the pain-inhibiting pathways in the brain.

A survey Mark and his colleagues conducted supports his theory that cold water is helping people by reducing inflammation. He put out a request for a response from people who considered themselves to be self-medicating with cold water swimming. Of the replies he received, two-thirds were swimming for mental health – the rest were for physical conditions. Of these, he noted, 'It was all the things we predicted. Stuff related to inflammation. Inflammatory bowel disease, fibromyalgia, PTSD, all these things. The list of things people came back saying they self-medicated for was identical to what we expected.'

11 The cold-water shock triggering of your sympathetic nervous system activates your fight or flight response. Stress hormones adrenalin and noradrenalin flush your body and your ventilation goes up. All this **makes you feel more alive**.

12 It stimulates what author Wallace J. Nichols has called our **'blue mind'**. In his popular TEDx talk, he observed, 'When we're with the water, it washes our troubles away. When we're standing at the sea, taking it in quietly it takes away our stress.' Researchers are increasingly showing there is something to this. BlueHealth, an interdisciplinary project funded by the European Commission, for instance, has found that short but regular time spent in blue spaces, such as a daily 20-minute walk along a seafront, cumulatively boosts long-term wellbeing.

13 Swim groups are **support groups**. There's something about the way we all have to look out for each other out there in the water, or even afterwards when warming up again, that can create an instant bond. As swim-advocate

Stacey Holloway told us in *Taking the Plunge*, 'Swimming in itself is quite a vulnerable thing to do. You're taking most of your clothes off for a start. You're often somewhere very public. Then you're getting into cold water, which is something where you really have to know your own body. It's risky. We've always got to be looking out for each other.'

14 Swimming can be an **adventure**. The hunt for a new swim spot, or even arriving at one you have never been to before, can make you feel like an amateur explorer, discovering a different world. Even places you think you know well can be transformed by weather or the seasons into something new.

15 You're **submerged in nature**, often on an eye-level with wildlife, from seabirds to seals. We found in our interviews that for many swimmers, this contact with nature was a key reason why they were there.

16 Expose your skin to sunlight and you can get **a Vitamin D fix**. The water may be chilly for most of the year, but for whatever time you are out there, particularly if you aren't wearing wetsuit, you are getting the sun's rays your skin and the benefits of all that tamin D.

17 It exercises your **circulation**. Cold water swimming is a brisk, rollercoaster workout for your circulatory system, prompting some vessels to dilate and constrict. It starts when cold water shock triggers the sympathetic nervous system to send more blood to vessels closer to the skin and your extremities, then shifts to sending it closer to your organs to protect them from the extreme cold and keep your core warm. The parasympathetic nervous system and the dive reflex are involved in that, in sending messages to shunt blood from our arms and legs to vital organs to keep them warm and oxygenated in extreme conditions.

It's been found that those who are adapted to cold water swimming have a more rapid limiting of blood flow to the skin, or vasoconstriction response. This ensures more heat is moved to the body, leaving the skin, hands and feet to cool but insulating the core. As Dr Heather Massey, cold water physiology researcher, has put it, 'This greater sensitivity to cold may also mean that it takes longer to rewarm your hands and feet compared to your friends who have not been cold exposed, as the blood vessels are slow to open and blood supply return to the fingers and toes.'

18 It lowers a chemical in your **blood** linked to heart disease. Homocysteine is a common amino acid in your blood, mostly derived from eating meat. High levels of it are linked to early development of heart disease.

19 Related to its other benefits, it can help **manage pain**. This is one of the reasons why cold water therapy is an increasingly popular sports treatment. According to medical experts, the reason cold water helps with pain is that it causes your blood vessels to constrict. This reduces blood flow to the area – for example, an injury you're applying ice to – which helps reduce swelling and inflammation. Research is still limited, but often cited is a BMJ case report into a 28-year-old man who suffered from post-operative pain and found it disappeared totally after doing an open water swim.

20 You are burning **plenty of calories**. A study performed at the University of Florida showed slightly more calories are burned in cold water exercise than in warm. It also increases your basal metabolic rate and could increase levels of brown fat, though further research is needed there.

21 **Anyone** can do it! The wild swimming community is fabulously inclusive, diverse and welcoming. There's no obligation to be super fit, an Olympic freestyle champion or in the first flush of youth . . . with none of the check-me-out swagger of the gym or anxiety of the unfamiliar exercise class, wild swimming is genuinely for everyone.

DON'T FORGET TO FLOAT

Many people die from sudden cold water immersion each year. Don't dive or jump suddenly into cold water, and if you do find yourself struggling with cold water shock, follow the RNLI advice to float for around 60 to 90 seconds – the time it takes for the effects of the shock of the cold water to pass and for you to regain control of your breathing.

Dorset

FLOAT LIKE A STARFISH

THE SAFE DIPPING CODE

This book is all about excitement and adventure, but let's not forget that being immersed in open water is a risky activity. Wherever you swim, whoever you're with and however experienced you are, we recommend you stick to the following code. That way you can stay safe and have fun!

1 Don't drink, or take drugs, and swim – in other words always swim sober. Just as with driving, for example, even small amounts of alcohol can impair your judgement.

2 If you're looking to try a new swim spot, source local knowledge on where is safe to go and check if any particular locations have specific risks.

3 Assess your environment carefully and make sure you have an exit point.

4 Check for risks like rip currents or river rapids. It is vital that you learn to recognise a rip current (see page 32).

5 Be aware of your own limits – this is a sign of true confidence. Just because someone thinks they can swim to the other side of the lake, it doesn't mean you can or that you need to try.

6 Be aware of the weather and tide times. Check the forecast so you're aware of what you may be dealing with and also, if you are sea swimming, the tides. If it's been raining recently, you should also recognise that rivers and waterfalls will be in spate and faster running, and that there may be more sewage, which has been allowed to outflow, in rivers and the sea.

7 Remember water can suddenly get deeper. What can seem like a shallow entry can suddenly shelve off, creating an entirely different swimming environment.

8 Don't jump or dive in until you have done a thorough risk assessment and know the water is deep enough and clear of obstructions. Failure to do this can result in life-changing injuries.

9 Don't try to rescue people in trouble. Raise the alarm at once. Dial 999 or 112 and ask for the Coastguard or relevant agency, to ensure trained professional rescue services are on their way. If

possible, throw something that floats into the water, or tell them to simply float, rather than try to swim.

10 Watch children at all times and be close enough to help them immediately.

11 Swim parallel to the shore rather than away from it.

12 Avoid swimming close to weirs. The area at the bottom of the falls can trap swimmers and hold them under the water.

13 Allow yourself to be seen. Wear a bright swim cap or use a tow float.

STAY SAFE.
FOLLOW THE SWIM SAFETY CODE

SPOT the dangers.

ADVICE – follow safety advice and read signs.

FRIEND – swim with others.

EMERGENCY call for help – recognise the signs of someone in trouble.

For more on water safety see outdoorswimmingsociety.com

BE DROWNING AWARE

WHAT DROWNING REALLY LOOKS LIKE

Learn to recognise the signs of drowning, which are not the thrashing around and shouting we often see in the movies.

A person drowning will tend to be upright, sometimes with head back and mouth open. Their eyes are likely to be panicked or glassy and empty. Long hair over the face can also be an indication. Sometimes people look as if they are climbing a ladder in the water, moving like this in an effort to stay buoyant.

IF SOMEONE LOOKS LIKE THEY ARE DROWNING

If you see someone you believe is drowning, don't jump in to rescue them, unless you are trained to do so.

Raise the alarm at once. Dial 999 or 112 and ask for the Coastguard or relevant agency, to ensure trained professional rescue services are on their way.

Shout and try to calm the struggling person and encourage them to stay afloat. If there is a life-ring or other public rescue equipment nearby, throw it to them. Do not attempt to rescue unless you have training to do so. The RNLI message is:

Call for help rather than endanger your own life and the lives of others.

IF YOU FALL IN THE WATER OR GET INTO TROUBLE

Remember, and tell everyone you know, that one of the RNLI's key messages is that if you find yourself struggling in the water you should 'float to live'. As they put it in their song written for kids, but applicable to us all, 'If you get in trouble just float like this; Use your arms and legs like a big starfish.'

The National Fire Chiefs Council runs a #bewateraware campaign. Their advice is that if you happen to unintentionally end up in the water, you should lie on your back and float, while shouting for someone to ring 999.

Llyn Geirionydd

LOCATING YOUR SWIM

For each spot, coordinates are given either for point of access or nearest car park. We have chosen to use what3words, available as an app or online at what3words.com. Be aware that things can change, so please do your own research beforehand.

There are many ways we could have given locations – GPS coordinates, Ordnance Survey references, postcodes – and we have both used all of these at different times. But for the purpose of this book, we chose what3words. We admit that was partly for the magic it brings to the page, and because its word poetry seems to chime with the spirit of wild swimming. If you would like to convert to GPS, you can do this either on the what3words app, or through their online convertor, what3words.com/products/batch-converter.

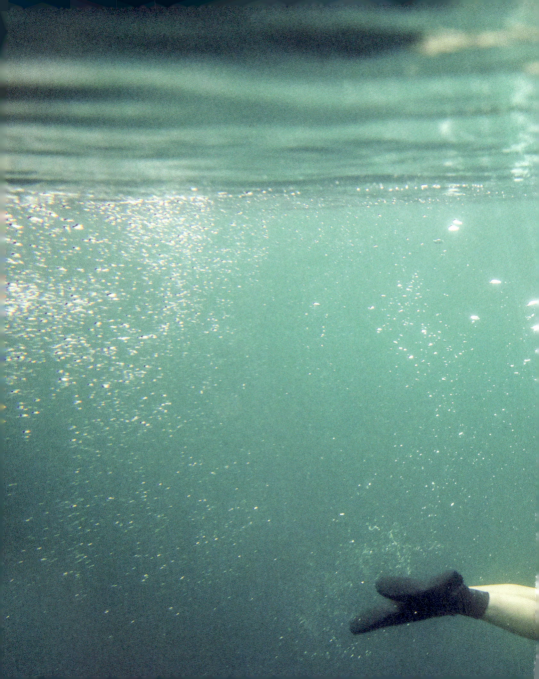

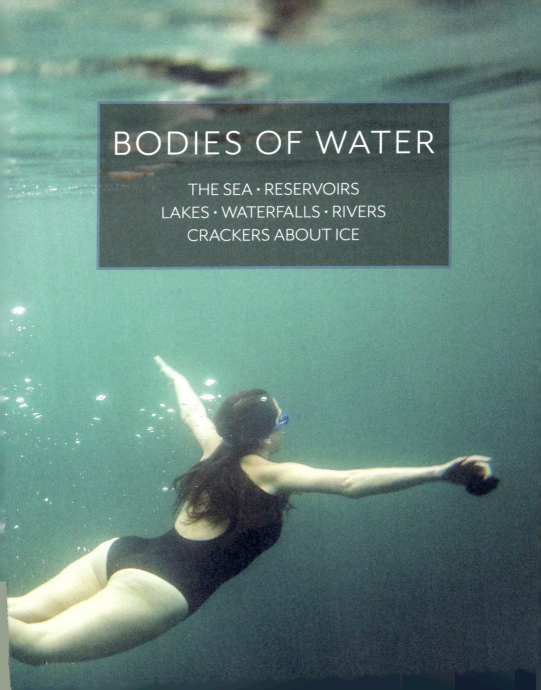

BODIES OF WATER

THE SEA · RESERVOIRS
LAKES · WATERFALLS · RIVERS
CRACKERS ABOUT ICE

Pedn Vounder

THE SEA

SALIM AHMED,
Shepperton
Open water swimming coach
SALIMSWIMLAB

I worked in the whisky trade and used to live in Scotland, before I became a full-time swimmer. I moved down to England about twenty years ago and, because I had been a competitive swimmer, started coaching at my son's school. I found this was something I loved, so I gave up my corporate life and went full-time as a coach, which soon became open water focused.

I set up Swim Lab in 2012. My focus was on developing the methodology that would harness the best of all the best methodologies out there, like total immersion and swim smooth. What I created was a six-point methodology for swimming, which was based on two key factors. One was body alignment and the other was how your body keeps evolving and changing with age and how you can adapt to it.

Swimming is a life journey and, in fact, it is one of the few things that you can – to some extent – actually get faster and swim further with as you age. That's because what you learn over time is how your body works, so your connection between your mind and your body becomes so much more fine-tuned. As you get older you learn how to deploy your strengths and weaknesses better. Whatever you lose in terms of muscle strength and VO2 max, is more than made up for by improvements in your technique and how to deploy them when you swim. I treat swimming as a performance art rather than a sport.

We should all have several programmes for swimming, such as one for open water without a wetsuit, in the sea with or without a wetsuit, in a pool without a wetsuit, in a lake with or without a wetsuit, and so on. These are all different settings you might need to have depending on what buoyancy you are likely to have in that type of water.

SIX WAYS TO RAISE YOUR SWIMMING GAME

1 Your hands should enter shoulder width apart as far away from your body as possible: so they stay shoulder width apart as you rotate. If you look at top swimmers, as opposed to those who have perhaps been taught at school, they'll have their hands shoulder width apart, as far away from the body as possible.

2 Head position should be looking down, to align the spine. Again the waterline should be cutting the middle of your head rather than your forehead, which goes against the grain of what we're often taught (which is to always look slightly forwards).

3 Feet and legs should be on the surface of the water behind us, just breaking the surface – and for endurance swimming not much more than that (because as little as 5 to 10 per cent of your forward propulsion comes from your legs). When you do use your legs, they use up a disproportionate amount of energy, so the maths doesn't support the overuse of your legs for endurance-level swimming. The idea is that you have your legs and feet in the right place, out of trouble, creating as little resistance as possible – which means they are on the surface, toes pointed and together.

4 I tell people to rotate from the hips rather than the shoulders. Imagine your spine is a broom handle rather than a flexible coil and your objective is to rotate on that broom handle. The gyroscopic effect of a body moving through the water spinning on its axis is what we're trying to create. Treat your entire body – from the tips of your fingers to the tips of your toes – as that which should be a straight line that rotates, and that you rotate on as you move through the water.

5 Swim with an 80% catch-up. Swimming with a 100% catch-up is when one arm completely comes round to catch up with the other before the other one goes. It's a brilliant training tip.

6 Keep your hand below the elbow on the recovery part of the stroke. This reduces lateral movement or minor snaking.

FIVE SEA SWIMMING POINTERS

1. Be buoyant, be brilliant

With sea swimming the first thing you need to think about is how buoyant you are because of the salt. You will automatically be on the surface more so than you would be in a lake or a pool. It's almost like wearing a wetsuit. That buoyancy is a

Praa Sands

key element in being able to swim with a minimal amount of effort – because a lot of the effort we make, especially to bring our legs up to the surface, involves kicking.

2. Keep in sight

The second thing to be aware of is the current as you go through the water. That's either something you have to fight against or something that will affect your direction. So sighting and learning how to adjust your direction as you swim becomes more important when you're in the sea, because otherwise you have no idea where you are.

The beauty of open water swimming, and the scariness of it, is that you might not know where you are. Unless you're swimming over a shallow reef and can see things below, you often have no measures to tell you that you are making any progress whatsoever. When you're in the deep sea away from the beach you can lose yourself in the water.

Being out in the vast ocean can bring on all those primal fears that can get into your head. Some people find it easier to swim in the sea than a lake; other people are absolutely terrified because you have nothing with which to orientate yourself.

I run trips to the Amalfi coast and Cornwall, and wherever I choose to do our open water swimming, I'm very conscious of what you see when you turn to

Sandsend

breathe. What you see when you swim is one of swimming's joys and is also what orientates you, be it the verdant hillsides of Positano or the grottos of Capri, these images make swimming truly mindful.

3. Tide times and rip currents

It's really important to understand tides and rips. Always assess where you are going to swim in the sea and work out where potential rip currents are. Also, decide what time of the day to swim, so you can find out whether the tide is coming in or out. This is vital: it's far more than just good housekeeping.

The reason rips need particular attention is because they are a body of water you can find yourself in which will simply sweep you out to sea. And the reaction we normally have as human beings, when we discover we're not making any progress against this rip current, is to panic and try to go faster against it. But this is exhausting, and that's when serious accidents happen. If you find yourself in a rip, I always advise people to do the counterintuitive thing of swimming obliquely with it, so you let the rip take you further out to sea, but at an angle. You want to swim out at 45 degrees to the direction of the rip. This feels counterintuitive, but will often help you swim back with more effectiveness.

Please always inform local lifeguards of your plans and never swim alone.

4. Become acclimatised

The key thing here is to do your homework. Generally the UK's west coast is going to be warmest around October and into November, so this can be a better time to swim than spring. Investigate, too, how currents may affect temperatures in the areas where you plan to swim.

Armed with that knowledge, what matters next is what you wear and how you prepare. It's about knowing your body and knowing how quickly you dissipate heat, which depends on training and exposure to cold water swimming. With open water swimming you need to learn to reach your optimum mobile temperature really quickly. When you start swimming, you lose heat straight away, but as you get to a certain pace and time in the water you generate heat, which eventually equals that.

A wetsuit speeds up all of that. You get warmer faster and you equalise much faster. If you swim in a wetsuit you get to that temperature much quicker and can swim much further using less energy. Wetsuits are great! Naturally, as you swim more, you will become acclimatised and able to wear fewer and fewer items.

5. Stung!

In warmer waters you will come across jellyfish more, but we get them in the UK too. They're why I tell people that learning a good breaststroke in open water makes excellent sense. Lord Byron did breaststroke for all his epic swims around the world. It's a fabulous stroke.

But the reason we do it when

> SOME PEOPLE FROWN ON WETSUITS. THERE'S A DEGREE OF SNOBBERY OUT THERE ABOUT SKINS VERSUS WETSUITS. I DON'T HAVE TIME FOR IT! DO WHAT MAKES YOU COMFORTABLE. SWIMMING IS NOT A COMPETITION IN 'HARD'-NESS.

we're in the Med is that it enables you to actually see the jellyfish. Often when you're doing front crawl you don't see them until they're right up next to you. If you find yourself surrounded by these aquatic menaces, do a controlled breaststroke and dodge.

WHY NOT CHECK OUT . . .

Man o' War Bay
📍 **indoors.violinist.gladiator**

A shingle beach on the east side of Durdle Door in Dorset, this is a beautiful spot and fairly safe to swim in because it shields a lot of the currents. You can swim there without seeing another soul.

CURRENT AFFAIRS

What do you need to know... about tides and currents?

Spring tides, when the sea has its biggest tidal range, happen when the sun, earth and moon are in a direct line, on a new moon or full moon. A neap tide, the smallest tidal range, occurs at the midpoint between these, on half moons.

The hour either side of a high or low tide is known as a slack tide, a period in which it can often seem as if the water is barely moving. Many people choose to swim on such tides.

Some parts of the country, such as the Bristol Channel, which has the world's second highest tidal range, have giant tidal ranges, which can leave you wading out a very long way if you arrive at anything other than high tide. Luckily for swimmers, Clevedon has a marine lake, a tidal pool, which holds onto the water and thus allows for swimming at other times of the day.

If you're trying out a new sea location ask experienced local swimmers, sailors and other knowledgeable experts about how the water behaves there. But also it's good to learn for yourself as much as you can about how water moves in the sea – and think about what those tides and currents might mean for you. Always check tide times and weather conditions before planning a swim.

What do you need to know... about jellyfish?

There are those who swim right through the winter in nothing but a swimming costume, yet are to be found donning their wetsuits like armour when summer comes and the jellyfish arrive. And not surprisingly. We may marvel at their beautiful, translucent floating forms, but none of us wants to get a sting from the trailing tentacles of a lion's mane *(cyanea capillata)*, which is the most dangerous common jellyfish in our waters. Its sting, which may at first only result in itching or mild localised pain, can start to radiate and result in pain in other areas of the body, progressing to back pain, nausea, abdominal cramps, sweating and hypertension.

More common than these, though, are the moon jellyfish, which sometimes wash in near our shores, which give no sting; the barrel jellyfish, a very mild stinger; and the compass jellyfish, whose sting is like being brushed by nettles.

What to do if you... get stung by a jellyfish?

The NHS website advises: 'Rinse the affected area with seawater (not fresh water). Remove any spines from the skin using tweezers or the edge of a bank card. Soak the area in very warm water (as hot as can be tolerated) for at least 30 minutes – use hot flannels or towels if you cannot soak it. Take painkillers like paracetamol or ibuprofen.' It also recommends that if you have severe pain that won't go away, or have been stung in the face or genitals, you should go to a minor injuries unit.

THREE TIPS ON TIME & TIDES

WILLIAM THOMSON
Tidal explorer and author of
The Book of Tides

🌐 TIDALCOMPASS.COM

1. A speed of knots

Timing your swims to make use of tidal streams will dramatically increase how far and fast you can swim. For example, if your usual 'speed through water' is 1 knot and the current is 2 knots, going with the flow will increase your 'speed over ground' to 3 knots, a 300 per cent speed boost! At this speed you would swim 3 nautical miles (5.55 kilometres) along the beach in just one hour – but if you tried swimming into the current, you would actually end up going backwards.

2. Cross-shore winds and slack waters

Tidal streams are currents that flow along the coast, and they change direction every six hours. This time is called 'slack water' and it is when the streams are slowest; after slack, they speed up for three hours and then slow down for three hours, changing direction again at the next slack water. With this in mind, if there is a cross-shore wind then you want to time your swim for when wind and water are heading in the same direction because the sea will be much smoother. In contrast, when wind and water are heading into each other the sea becomes very choppy and uncomfortable for swimming. There's nothing worse than getting slapped in the face by a cold wave just as you come up for air!

3. A shorebreak strategy

Steep, sloping beaches will experience dangerous dumping waves called a 'shorebreak' – swimmers want to avoid these at all costs.

A simple tactic is to stand patiently on the beach and wait for the set of waves to pass, then quickly swim out into the deeper

Treyarnon Bay

water beyond the 'surf zone' before the next set arrives. Because waves break in shallow water, being in deeper water will keep you safe from the steep breaking waves. On your way back in, swim to just outside the surf zone and follow the same routine in reverse, waiting for a set to pass and then quickly swimming back to shore before the next set comes.

FIND OUT MORE . . .

- **The Book of Tides**. Read the book or watch the videos on the Tide School YouTube channel.
- **The Willy Weather app**. Used by fisherfolk, it tells you about weather, tides and swells at your location.

Langset Reservoir

RESERVOIRS

Hang on . . . reservoirs? But swimming in them isn't allowed, is it?

Well, that is partially true, for many reservoirs. Advice on the Outdoor Swimming Society website states, 'Reservoirs are usually owned by water companies, and they have a legal duty to provide public access for recreation to the land and water, though in practice most have a No Swimming rule and notices.'

But there are campaigns to change this. And, as the OSS points out, there are very good reasons why swimming should be allowed. Owen Hayman is among those activists fighting for reservoir swimming. Here is his guide to swimming in the reservoirs of Yorkshire Water and other areas. Bear in mind that these are his opinions and experiences and he has an agenda. He wants to provoke change! If that's something you're interested in too, then read on . . .

OWEN HAYMAN
Horticulturist & Outdoor Swimming Society inland access officer
OWAINHAEMAN

I often swim in Yorkshire Water reservoirs. Thanks to the widely spread fear-inducing untruths about reservoirs, and the dark peaty colour of water flowing from peak moorlands that fill them around Sheffield, for most people there is something particularly intimidating about these places. Only three years ago, it was still a surprising and sometimes shocking thing to see swimmers in reservoirs in the area.

However, in the past few years, the general public seems to be coming around to the idea that reservoirs are not necessarily swirling whirlpools of pipes and machinery, but hugely undervalued blue spaces.

Accurate information and positive experiences are helping to overcome the fear, as people try it for themselves and begin to understand how other countries see most reservoirs simply as lakes, with a dam wall and tower to avoid when swimming. And now thousands of people are seeing these seemingly dark industrial reservoirs with their intimidating dam walls through new eyes. But, still, we are technically trespassing. A responsibility-focused community is growing to make sure we foster swimmers as stewards of the environment, not simply users of it.

There are around 2,000 reservoirs in England and Wales, with huge potential to meet rising demand as open water swimming surges in popularity. Free informal outdoor swimming is seeing a huge and growing increase in popularity, and issues related to overuse and overcrowding of swim spots are becoming more common.

Some functioning reservoirs have free open swimming access (e.g. Sparth Reservoir, Huddersfield), and there is free open access for swimming at some disused reservoirs too (e.g. National Trust's Carding Mill Valley Reservoir, Shropshire). Countless functioning reservoirs are the base for formal open water swimming clubs (e.g. Harthill Reservoir, Rotherham).

RESERVOIR SWIM SAFETY

In Scotland, the Land Reform Act 2003 made reservoirs accessible for swimming. This doesn't apply to England and Wales, but their simple safety advice is invaluable:

- Access from a shallow area – do not enter by, or swim near, the reservoir structures, including dam wall, towers

Watershallows Reservoir

THE ART OF WILD SWIMMING: ENGLAND & WALES

or spillways. Tower sluices have undertows which can pull you under.
- NEVER jump from the dam towers – people have died by being sucked under by reservoir sluices.

Away from the tower, overflow and any other infrastructure, reservoirs are free from the hazards associated with rivers and the sea. There is generally no perceivable flow, current or tides. Despite common misinformation that reservoirs are very cold, the upper depths in which people swim are no colder than in comparable natural lakes. At some times of the year they are warmer than rivers or the sea. When you take into account the risk associated with travelling long distances to the sea, the risks involved in swimming in a local reservoir are considerably lower.

THE LEGALITY OF RESERVOIR SWIMMING

Is it illegal to swim . . . in Yorkshire Water reservoirs?

Byelaws do prohibit swimming in Yorkshire Water (YW) reservoirs (Water Park Byelaws 2010). However, these may not stand if the byelaws are not signed at the site, which is the case at the vast majority of YW reservoirs, so do your own research on this.

It is worth noting that many byelaws do not stand up in court. For example, there are byelaws that aim to make listening to an mp3 player, climbing a tree, washing your car, or using offensive language on YW sites a criminal offence.

The Water Industry Act 1991 Section 3 (5) states that water companies must 'ensure that the water or land is made available for recreational purposes and is so made available in the best manner'. While many reservoirs have footpaths, fishing and boating, swimming is often neglected. All these byelaws can change, however; it's possible they may become more tightly or differently enforced.

What to do if you're . . . asked to get out of a reservoir?

When swimming in Yorkshire Water reservoirs you may be asked to get out by YW staff, contracted security staff, Peak District National Park rangers, or South Yorkshire Fire & Rescue. They are just doing their job, and will generally be polite, but may tell you fear-mongering stories!

Always be calm and civil in return. You have two options in this situation.

1 Comply and get out of the water. They may leave you alone and you can choose to get back in once they've gone.

2 Politely decline their request to get out the water. They may call the police if you do this. If the police arrive and order you to get out, it would be best

Langset Reservoir

to do so, as there could be a risk of arrest. But the police do not seem to take this approach in Sheffield. In my experience they do not attend calls about adult swimmers, nor do they threaten them with arrest. This could, of course, change!

What more do you need... to know about byelaws?

As I understand it, Yorkshire Water can only bring about a prosecution using their Byelaw Enforcement Policy, which is almost impossible for them to follow through. My understanding is that only if you've found yourself at the stage where you've been caught four times and your name and address taken each time, and you've been sent three formal letters, can YW even consider prosecuting you.

To find out if there are byelaws at a reservoir, and any associated byelaw prosecution procedure, check the website of the company that owns or manages the reservoir. Failing that, email them to ask.

Bear in mind that many byelaws are untested in court – it might be that they wouldn't stand up. In fact, many well-established and seemingly undisputed swim spots are covered by byelaws that criminalise swimming among other activities. Some of which seem a little obscure and strange. For example, YW's byelaws make it a criminal offence to arrive via parachute or play a musical instrument at their reservoirs.

How can you... support change around access?

- Sign the Clear Access Clear Waters campaign petition.
- Join the Right to Roam campaign.
- Download the free Inland Bathing Areas guide, to setting up inland bathing areas in the UK, from the Outdoor Swimming Society website.
- Join the Outdoor Swimming Society Inland Access Group on Facebook.
- Read online the OSS's '16 Reasons for Swimming Access in Reservoirs'.

WHY NOT CHECK OUT...

Sparth Reservoir, Huddersfield
📍 **strut.disco.mulls**

A top-up reservoir for a canal, this small body of water was the site of a vital and very interesting access campaign, and is thus a legendary swim spot in the Yorkshire area. Despite the fact the reservoir had been widely used by the local community for swimming since at least the 1940s, 'No Swimming' signs went up in 2011. A long access campaign ensued until success in 2017. The site is now totally open access and seen as the perfect model.

Wastwater

LAKES

GILLY MCARTHUR,
Lake District
Rock climber & illustrator
GILLYMCARTHUR

What I like best about freshwater swimming is that every day you have a changing water-level view. There is a connection with nature which feels more heightened than swimming in the sea. What I have discovered with lake swimming is the beautiful pattern of the year, of birth to death to rebirth. It's reassuring – a cycle of life quietly playing out under our bare feet.

A yearly cycle of plants and birds
In early spring there is a heady scent of wild garlic; the moist acidic soils of the wood here are incredible in enabling it to thrive and everyone has a glut of pesto in their fridges!

Graceful wings which announce the start of summer are always a welcome sight, with the swifts and swallows arriving from overseas to the small stone boathouse.

A yellow tint on the chestnut trees suggests autumn is waiting offstage. These trees are always the first to turn and on the far-off shore the deciduous forest slowly changes from emerald green to yellow then. As the bracken dies back you know winter will soon arrive.

By November the water drops below 10°C and you can see your breath for the first time. The trees, now stark and bare, make the lake surface awash with leaves (hiding monsters beneath?). It's time to think about bobble hats and sharing cake recipes again.

Winter is peaceful, cool and starkly beautiful. Life is still there, but it's harder to find.

Maintaining nature's majesty
Alongside the beauty is the ugly cycle of litter, scorched earth from BBQs, smashed

glass and broken weeping tree limbs from vandalism on the shoreline. Summer brings crowds of people, perhaps new to the lake and unaware of this fragile ecosystem. I prefer winter when there are fewer people.

We all have a debt to pay if we wish to engage in the outdoors; the outdoors is not free. The fee is respect for Mother Nature. She doesn't ask for much from us: just to collect litter, tread carefully and hold the space delicately. If we all do our bit, maybe she has a chance to keep being majestic as the seasons pass for years to come.

WHY NOT CHECK OUT . . .

Wastwater
📍 funny.aliens.canyons

I love Wastwater because it is remote, deep and cold all year round. Even when Windermere is sitting at 20°C, this body of water takes no prisoners. It feels very adventurous swimming here. There is no phone signal, no public transport and it was only in the 1970s that the valley got electricity. It's also literally a dead-end.

Wastwater is about three miles long. It sits, pristine and dramatic, in the western lakes. As a swimmer, you understand and respect how pristine this water is. If you swim here you absolutely must check your kit before you enter for invasive species.

What makes this water so special is the mountainscape and screws that descend deep into the water on all sides. As a rock climber, I have written about Scafell Pike – its rugged handsome beauty. The tallest mountain in England, it's a climber's paradise. The rock-climbing in this part of the Lake District is engrossing, technical and adventurous; much like a swim here. The water shelves to a depth of over 70 metres and can feel intimidating. But after a day on the summit, to come down to the valley floor and finish the day with a swim is nothing short of magical.

At the end of the water sits the Wasdale Head – a climbers' pub and walkers' bar, with a great range of ales and history in abundance (plus the most uncomfortable seats!). This, like the climbing and swimming, makes this a valley to check out. Bring a bag of time. It's a beauty.

A NOTE ON LAKE SWIM SAFETY

More than 85% of fatal drownings occur at open water sites. Many of these are attributed to lack of understanding and knowledge of the hazards of open water, especially the cold. Research the location you intend to swim at. Go there several times and in different weather conditions. Or join a group that already knows the lake well and swims there regularly.

Wastwater

SWIM COACH SARAH WISEMAN'S BIG QUESTIONS TO ASK BEFORE YOU GET IN A LAKE

- Is it accessible? How will you arrive there?
- When you arrive at your spot watch the water for a while. What is it doing? How does it move? How does it behave?
- Does the body of water have a flow or a movement? Is it tidal? If so, how fast is it moving?
- What hazards can you see? Are there any rocks or trees nearby? Do they look stable?
- What colour is the water?
- Does the water look clean?
- Can you tell how deep the water is?
- Can you see safe places to get in and out of the water?
- What will you do if something goes wrong?
- Do you know the location's address or a grid reference (or what3words) to give to emergency services?
- Lastly, have you thought where you will leave your belongings?

WATERFALLS

JONATHAN COWIE,
Kendal
Editor, Outdoor Swimmer
JONNYHCOWIE

The force and joy of waterfalls

Stunningly beautiful, waterfalls are the playgrounds of wild swimming, with deep pools, cliffs to jump off and the torrent of water that is the fall or force (from 'fors', the Old Norse for waterfall). Nothing beats the thrill of leaping off the edge of a waterfall into a deep pool below.

Waterfalls are found in the upper courses of rivers, often hidden in valleys in mountainous areas. There is something secretive and magical about them, and many have folklore tales associated with them. I have loved falls since I was a kid when a walk to High Force and Low Force in Teesdale was a favourite day out.

How can you ...
stay safe in a waterfall?

A waterfall in full spate is an awe-inspiring sight, but fast-moving water brings with it its own dangers and each waterfall must be risk assessed before swimming or jumping. As waterfalls usually form when rivers are still young, the water can be colder than further downstream, so be aware of cold water shock.

Fast-flowing water can cause currents and eddies, especially when flowing around rocks, so check before entering that there is no risk of being swept downstream or becoming stuck on rocks. If you are thinking of swimming under it, beware of the force of the fall: don't get trapped by the weight of the water.

Jumping off a waterfall into the pool below is one of life's greatest pleasures, but check for obstructions and depth first even if you have jumped there before. Waterfalls vary in force depending on the season and rainfall, which means water levels at jumping spots can change.

Tal y Bont Waterfalls

WHY NOT CHECK OUT...

Black Moss Pot, Borrowdale
📍 breeze.aced.bands

This spot in the Langstrath Valley is one of my favourite places to swim. Here it is not the falls but the deep gorge that is the star of the show – a wild swimmer's playground where you can while away hours jumping off rocks into the gorge or letting the strong current whisk you downstream. Get there early for a cheeky skinny dip!

Park in the National Trust car park at Rosthwaite or in Stonethwaite by the phone box and walk up the valley. It's a decent hike but so worth it.

River Wey, Newark

RIVERS

ELLA FOOTE,
Surrey
Journalist & dip advisor
ELLACHLOESWIMS

I am an experienced outdoor swimmer, certified open water lifeguard, STA swim teacher, open water coach and swimming journalist. An intrepid swim explorer, I am constantly seeking out new rivers, lakes, ponds, seas and pools to plunge into. I am contributing editor at *Outdoor Swimmer* magazine, an event speaker, year-round outdoor swimmer and happy doing distance or dips. Every day I have a reason to put on a swimsuit and I wouldn't have it any other way!

Going with the flow – the joy of river swimming

Rivers have been written into verses of poetry, lines in literature, melodies in music and painted onto canvas. There are popular riverside walking paths and historic navigational routes. Often tarnished as dirty and unsafe for swimming, rivers can get bad press. But here's the thing about a river: what flows through today will be gone tomorrow. Unlike the sea or a large lake, a river reflects seasonal changes, with wildlife, weeds, flower and fauna like no other waterway. In winter, many rivers can look bleak, brown and fast flowing. But if you are submerged and your eyes are level with the roots and earth of the riverbank, you can see the beginnings of the next spring, reminding you that beauty often follows the dark.

Spring offers revival and hope, with an abundance of blooms and blossom. Swans tug at brown dead reeds from the riverbed and collect winter driftwood for their nests as leaves unfurl on trees. Shallow riverbeds on bends start to sprout slithery, thick roots underfoot, they can surprise and scare the new swimmer with their snake-like appearance, but if you are a river swimmer you recognise the winding path of the lily-pad plants as a

sign of warmer weather to come. Mayflies and mist over the water is a midsummer special and the heat of July brings stinging nettles to entry and exit points, giving bare skin an unwanted tingle. Shallow rivers in August produce long hair-like reeds that brush against legs. In autumn the cries from Canadian geese and low-flying synchronised flocks signal the click into cooler weather and shorter days.

If you want to really wild swim, choose a river. It will offer a wild ride on its current, slide you around its natural curves and spit you out into a brackish estuary. The sinking mud will suck at your toes and brambles will offer blackberries to snuffle on your way. Swim upstream and keep yourself warm in winter with a natural workout like no other, float on your back and gaze at the moon on a warm summer's night. Find a river's source and walk its course until deep enough for a dip, clamber under waterfalls and plunge into rocky pools of young clear water.

Those of us who have read *The House at Pooh Corner* have an appreciation of the way in which rivers are grown-ups, more self-aware than childish streams.

TEN RIVER SWIMMING TIPS

1 Never swim in flooded rivers or rivers in spate. If a river is high and fast flowing, it is best to avoid. Think about water quality. Avoid swimming after heavy rains, particularly in areas close to sewage outfalls, where there may be high concentrations of waste. The Rivers Trust have created an interactive map of sewage discharges into England's rivers which allows swimmers to choose to avoid swimming directly downstream of them after heavy rain. Check also for blue-green algal blooms.

2 Before you get in, take a look at proper look at the river and identify where the current runs fastest, or where it looks shallow or deep. Throw sticks or leaves in to check the speed of the flow. The main current of a river is usually in its centre or on its outside bend.

3 Make sure you have an exit plan before you get in. If swimming in a river pool try to get in and out where the water runs shallow and swim upstream before you go downstream. This way if you are pushed any further downstream you will get beached and it will still be easy to get out. If swimming from point to point, thoroughly check your exit point as well as your entry point before you get in.

4 Check for obstructions and hazards before you get in and take care when swimming. It is easy to bash your ankle or knee on a submerged rock, fallen branch or a sunken jetty or platform. Protect your feet with neoprene socks or shoes.

5 Avoid weirs and locks. Box weirs can be fatal for swimmers and kayakers. Do not slide down the face of a weir as the bottom of the falls is the area of greatest danger. Locks impact swimmers with their moving water, currents and boat traffic. Plus, it is very hard to exit them.

6 Fallen trees, undercuts and tree roots are dangerous. If you want to jump or dive in, it is essential that you get into the water first and carefully test the depth of the area and ensure it is fully clear of hazards. Swim under and take a look with your goggles on. Never assume that because somewhere is known as a local diving spot that it will be safe on the day you go. There may not be sufficient depth, or rocks and branches may have moved into what was previously a safe entry spot.

7 Weil's disease, or leptospirosis, is much talked about but rare. To mitigate the risks cover cuts with waterproof dressings and avoid stagnant water. If flu-like symptoms develop within 1 to 3 weeks of swimming see your doctor. Be sure to wash your hands after swimming.

8 Be aware of other river users – kayakers, rowers, other boats and fisherfolk. Wear a bright cap or use a tow float and, if possible, make the other users aware of you. Swim wide of people fishing and watch out for lines.

9 Learn everything you can about biosecurity – see page 63.

10 Remember that access to a stretch of river is only permitted in England and Wales if there is a public footpath or highway, or permission has been established with the landowner. Otherwise, it is technically a trespass (see page 65).

WHY NOT CHECK OUT . . .

River Dart
📍 **gazes.penny.sometime**

I love this river because it offers such a huge range of swimming on its course from Dartmoor down to the sea. Head into Dartmoor National Park from the A38 at Ashburton and find car parks, walking trails, dipping points and large rocks to lie on after a cool swim. Water is the colour and clarity of Coca-Cola in summer; it is a great adventure for all ages.

Further downstream near Staverton the river widens and deepens for longer, proper swimming. It offers lengths of swimming on the straights so long as the weather hasn't been too wet, otherwise it is too fast. Downstream of Totnes you need to check the tides, or you can find yourself knee-deep in mud. The water is a briny mix of freshwater and sea salt.

FENWICK RIDLEY ON RIVER ETIQUETTE

THE FIRST BIG RULE OF ENTERING THE WATER IS TO COMMUNICATE WITH OTHER USERS. IF THERE ARE SOME ROWERS, WAIT UNTIL THEY COME DOWN AND THEN YOU CAN SAY, FOR EXAMPLE, 'IS IT ALL RIGHT IF I COME IN ON THE LEFT HAND SIDE, I'VE GOT MY TOW FLOAT?' HAVE THAT COMMUNICATION!

REBECCA WARD ON LOOKING AFTER THE RIVER YOU LOVE

How can you help... care for a local river?

Every area has its own microcosm of different wildlife. As a river conservation volunteer, I encourage swimmers to be custodians of where they swim. I like to see a well-loved and well-supported stretch of river. If I arrive at a river in which everything is flourishing and in balance, I notice it. I notice when it has had positive human intervention. You can tell when it's being managed, when a river keeper is looking after a stretch.

Every local Rivers Trust maintains stretches of river, keeps them clean, fosters wildlife habitats and does all the things I thought Mother Nature did herself. What I discovered is that if somebody doesn't get involved in creating those conditions you end up with a barren stretch of river or it just becomes overgrown with plants competing for space. It becomes too shady, not enough light gets into the water. But you don't want too much sunlight either, because that's how you end up with an overgrowth of bacteria.

How can you... be visible, be heard?

The groups I swim with do litter picks; we pick up our own rubbish and that of others. Yes, it can feel like you're picking up for other people. But we're the ones who are seen in the water. You're very visible with a bright orange float in the water in the middle of December! It's really important for people to see you picking up litter and protecting the environment. It builds a good perception of us as swimmers.

I don't see water companies as the bad guys. They have a vested interest in protecting the water. But, once you start swimming, you can use your voice to create change. You do have a responsibility, particularly if you're on social media. It's great posting photos of yourself in your swimsuit, but if you've got a following use your influence positively.

You care for what you have a passion for. Once you do something for leisure, then you're not simply a passive viewer any more. You've been in that water, around it, literally submersed in it, so you want to learn about it and look after it.

FENWICK RIDLEY ON THE ART OF RIVER TREKKING

As a pioneering river trekker, one of my biggest adventures was a river trek up the North Tyne, swimming, walking and following the length of the river from Newcastle to Kielder, scaling it in seven days with a RuckRaft. It was an absolute beast, a real teacher of a challenge. For those who would like to try river trekking, I'm delighted to share these six tips.

1 Learn the river as much as you can before you start trekking up it.

2 Wear the right gear. I protect my arms and legs and all over because I fall down a lot. I wear a swim-run wetsuit and if I'm in faster, bigger water, I'll wear a full suit. I always wear neoprene boots – and mine are huge, big diving boots that give support.

3 Be prepared for bruises. It's going to hurt and you're going to fall over a lot.

4 Take a walking pole. I use a nice stick that my dad's cut up. I don't like using walking poles in the river because they break and then you have to put them in the bin.

5 Take a RuckRaft to carry your stuff. For adventure swimming, going up the Tyne and going into the lakes, hands down one of the best things you can use is the RuckRaft. When Above Below created them they fixed what had been a big problem for me! I'd been crying out for this piece of kit; it creates a completely different level of wild swimming adventures. I'm aiming to do a night adventure swim with the RuckRaft soon, which I'm very excited about.

6 Don't swim in flood water. Me and my stomach have definitely adapted to some nasty bodies of water, but I certainly wouldn't swim in flood water. It's just not healthy to jump into a flood river. Even when the river is not in flood, there's also the danger side of things. You have branches that come down. When I did my trek up the river, Tyne Travel mission, I swam into things. You can break a finger, smash your teeth off something. Don't swim in flooded water!

DID YOU KNOW?
Citizen science research led by Swansea University academics found that 99% of river basins in the UK are fragmented by artificial barriers like dams, weirs and culverts.

CRACKERS ABOUT ICE

Sweethope Lough

FENWICK RIDLEY,
Corbridge, Northumberland
Cold water coach &
river trekker

🌐 H2OTRAILS.CO.UK

Ice swimming is classified as getting into water that is less than 5°C. It is important to address some of its pros and cons, its dangers, as well as what kit is needed for ice swimming. I feel one thing that's not talked about enough is that this is an extreme thing to do and put your body though. Preparation is key, and that includes making sure you've got the right equipment with you.

The biggest thing to heed about ice swimming, especially for someone who is new to it, is not to do it by yourself. You must go with people who have already done it and have done a few winter seasons. Not just one – that's not experience, that's dabbling. Even better, hire a cold water coach – someone who can deliver you a course and offer sure guidance and support, who can deliver that lovely building of acclimatisation and experience. Get that and you'll become an ice swimmer in no time.

How can you . . . cut an ice hole?

I've made a YouTube video on ice holes which you might find worth a watch. Ice channels, ice holes . . . both are fairly dangerous. You shouldn't be making an ice hole if the ice is less than 3 to 4 inches thick. You also shouldn't be walking on ice without the correct knowledge and the ability to check the thickness of the ice. I tend to cut the hole with an axe, but if you're not very confident with an axe, you shouldn't take one. It's all about being safe, and axes in uncertain or inexperienced hands can be very dangerous.

What do you need . . . before you enter the water?

You will need to have all the right clothing with you and make sure your gear is tip top. You should also make sure your clothes and towel are all laid out for when you emerge from the water.

You should be aware of the big changes going on in your body when you get in the cold water. These are different for each person. Some of us can acclimatise a lot quicker than others – and some people will find that cold water shock will come in a bit more dramatically than for others. And it probably will frighten them.

How should you . . . best start off?

My approach is to start slow and not expect to stay in very long. As you go in, control your breathing, keep it nice and slow. Focus on your breathing, not the swimming. Once you have got your breathing sorted and you're fully in the water, then you can start thinking about moving around. Keep it very short to begin with. Ignore those minutes-to-temperature charts – they are awful to hear about and, to my mind, don't make any sense. Keeping that time period low at the beginning is absolutely key.

What should you do . . . when you come out of the water?

I've noticed that a lot of people get out of the water and start running around to warm up rather than drying themselves straight away. Please, don't do that! Go straight to the gear, get the towel, pat yourself dry rather than rub yourself. (If you rub yourself that can cause a bit of problem with skin and irritation.) Get those layers on. Three layers, four layers: yeah, man, get them all on. Cocoon yourself. Get yourself a warm drink.

Rydal Waterfalls

Small Water

HOW TO BE AN AWESOME WILD SWIMMER

CODES OF CONDUCT

The true art of wild swimming, we believe, isn't just about where you swim, what strokes you use, what you wear, or even what you put in your flask – it's an attitude, a state of mind, of connection and caring for the watery places and ecosystems that give us such pleasure. More and more swimmers are talking about this feeling of consideration and interdependece. Some have even come up with outdoor swimming codes. We feel these tips by Gilly McArthur sum it all up.

TAKE RESPONSIBILITY AS A WILD SWIMMER

- **Check access** – not all bodies of water are swimmable and safe.
- **Park responsibly** – don't squash verges, block farm gates or park in passing places. Sheep and tractors need space!
- **Be biosecurity aware** (more of that shortly) and alert to cross-contamination. Protect the habitats you swim in. Remember the simple mantra: Check. Clean. Dry.
- **Pick up litter** every single time you swim. Even if it's not yours and even if it's tiny.
- **Leave no trace** – it goes without saying, but if you forget your bra and pants go back for them.
- **Be sensitive to locals** and homes nearby in terms of noise levels – especially early morning squeals.
- **Be inquisitive** to find new safe swim spots – seek out OS maps, books and local swim groups or guide knowledge. Some places should be kept secret – not every spot needs to be promoted on social media. Overused spot? Swim elsewhere – you will love it more!
- **Be kind and considerate** to other water users and shore walkers and learn about your local swim spot. Get to know it and love it over the year as the seasons unfold.

GILLY MCARTHUR'S GUIDE TO BIOSECURITY

As wild swimmers, we also don't want to be responsible for transferring invasive and harmful species between swim locations. To do this we need to take certain precautions.

Across the UK there is deadly work at play. Invasive species, mostly introduced in Victorian times for aquariums and gardens, are now playing havoc within our natural habitats.

Biosecurity is an untalked about issue in the swimming world.

With the increase in swimmers taking to lakes, rivers and bodies of water for their mental and physical wellbeing it's important to talk about it now.

Dangling off our costumes and hidden under goggle straps and the buckles of water shoes are aliens which could be far more devastating than we realise!

Just a tiny 2mm sprout of New Zealand pigmyweed poses a significant threat to an entire lake.

All is not lost, however, and education and awareness are key. It's really very simple. What you need to do is remember these three simple actions:

CHECK. CLEAN. DRY.

If you are going to swim in different bodies of water in a day, you must take different costumes with you; this is by far the easiest way to stop the scourge of invasive species.

If this isn't possible, you must check your costume, wetsuit, paddleboard, water shoes and hair between waters. Check for alien hitch-hikers, clean under velcro and watch straps, and dry the items that have been in the water before moving on.

ACCESS WHICH AREAS?

IMOGEN RADFORD: A SWIMMER'S GUIDE TO ACCESS, SAFETY AND RESPONSIBILITY

As one of the Outdoor Swimming Society's Inland Access team I seek to improve access based on shared understandings of swim safety and responsibilities. I advise campaigners and talk to local and national landowners and authorities.

People have always splashed around in their local river, but recently many more have become outdoor swimmers. Finding somewhere they are allowed to swim without hassle can be hard, as 'No Swimming' and 'Stay Out' messages litter riverbanks and information online. This can put people off, especially those already less likely to use the countryside: minoritised communities, urban dwellers, new swimmers, and anyone vulnerable or with mental health issues. It can drive some to swim in hidden, less suitable places and for them, possibly, to be less safe.

What do you need . . . to know about access?

The law on access to swim in rivers and lakes is complex and disputed. Unless you reach the water by public footpath or accepted access, it is trespass if you cross private land. There are strong arguments that there are common law rights to public navigation, including swimming in rivers, but some dispute this. Landowners own half of the riverbed and sometimes say this means swimmers cannot pass along the river. But they don't own the water.

I believe we need better, clearer legislation, which legalises the right to roam our waterways and offers more places to access the water from the banks.

What do you need . . . to know about risk?

Crucial to extending and protecting access is countering the misunderstandings of landowners and authorities about their potential liability and the safety of swimmers. Many believe they could be successfully sued if someone was injured or drowned while swimming. However, it is well established in case law that we swim at our own risk, and the landowner would only be liable if they fail to assess the risks and warn of any unusual or unseen hazards.

Crucial, too, is giving swimmers accurate information about those common risks and how they can avoid harm. It isn't the landowner's responsibility to do that, but it would be good practice to liaise with swimmers to give clear, simple advice, especially if they know people unfamiliar with swimming are entering the water.

Landowners and authorities don't want anyone to come to harm, and so they might think they can keep people safe by keeping them out of the water. But that is perhaps an unrealistic mindset; if people want to get in, they will – and surely they should have the opportunity to enjoy this healthy, affordable and fun activity.

What can you do . . . to be part of the solution?

There are too few places inland where people can access water when demand is high and this has led to concerns about overcrowding and negative impacts on communities and the environment. Part of the solution to this problem is surely to have more places where people can go.

The other part is for landowners and swimmers to work together to promote responsible, safe and considerate swimming. Swimmers keen to protect the places they swim can help the landowner manage problems like litter, report problems and be a positive influence in helping to raise awareness. Equally, landowners could provide clear information and signage, and work with local authorities and swimmers in setting up education sessions.

Working together like this would allow more people to swim in more places, to do so safely and to do so while respecting and caring for the places where they swim and the communities that surround them.

WANT TO FIND OUT MORE?

For advice on access and legality: outdoorswimmingsociety.com/is-it-legal

For a guide to landowners on establishing swimming places, with good practice examples and case law see: outdoorswimmingsociety.com/access-all-areas

The Clear Access Clear Waters campaign works to achieve fair, shared and sustainable open access to waterways for swimmers and other water users. Find out more at: clearaccessclearwaters.org.uk

WHERE THE WILD THINGS ARE

For many of us, the aquatic life – the seaweed, the wildfowl, the passing seals – are as much a reason for us to be there as the water. But, as we are splashing around marvelling at the living wonders all around, we also need to be careful about the impact we are having on their worlds.

Please consider this wildlife etiquette checklist:

- **Keep a lookout** in the water for nearby wildlife and be aware of its movements.
- **Do not approach** wild marine life or deliberately swim head on at it. Let any encounter be on their terms.
- **Make steady and predictable movements** and be prepared to move out of the animal's way.
- **Don't chase wildlife** or separate or scatter it.
- **Be quiet** – avoid making a lot of noise.
- **Allow an escape route** if you are a large group swimming in the water.
- **Do not approach mothers** with young.
- **Tread lightly** and be careful of where you put your feet – some species are vulnerable to physical damage.
- **Do not feed wild animals** – this can have damaging lifelong effects.

What to do if you . . . meet a seal while swimming?

Remain quiet, steady and assertive in the water. Seals are highly intelligent, similar to dogs, and good at reading your body language. If for some reason you are bitten or scratched by a seal – or if your skin is broken by a seal in any way – you are advised to seek medical advice and take a special form of antibiotics.

How do you report . . . a stranded marine mammal?

Rescue for live strandings can be called 24 hours a day through British Divers Marine Life Rescue (BDMLR) on 01825 765546, or contact them via bdmlr.org.uk.

For details on how to report a dead stranding, please see strandings.org.

WILDLIFE AT HEART

KATIE MAGGS,
Penzance
College deputy & health sciences lecturer, BDMLR marine mammal medic

TONICOFTHESEA

I am a snorkeller and sea swimmer based in Penzance. My journey with sea swimming began in 2017 when I suffered a breakdown through modern-day burnout. I developed crippling fatigue and anxiety.

I had spent most of my time as a young child with my dad – diving, swimming and snorkelling in and around local hidden Cornish coves. It was this rediscovery of absolute joy and wonder at being in the ocean that saved me. Post-recovery, I was extremely lucky to have a BAFTA-nominated short film made about my journey with mental health, *Tonic of the Sea*, which you can watch on YouTube. Now I provide motivational talks on the power of spending regular time immersed in some form of nature.

Alongside my daily dawn swimming I am a keen snorkeller and I greatly enjoy my marine life photography. Snorkelling around the Cornish coastline all year round has taken me on many an incredible journey where I have rediscovered my childlike curiosity for Cornwall's marine megafauna and flora.

While swimming and snorkelling, I regularly encounter a diverse variety of marine species that come and go throughout the seasons. I am lucky enough to have been joined by inquisitive grey seals, basking sharks and my favourite creature in the ocean to photograph – the jellyfish. We encounter a few different species here in Cornwall, usually beginning in late May and lasting until late September. Each year I swim beside blue, crystal, compass, comb, moon and barrel jellyfish, alongside colonial organisms such as the Portuguese man o' war and *velella velella* – more commonly known as 'by the wind sailors'.

How can you . . . take care of seals?

Driven by my love, enthusiasm and respect for ocean life, I qualified as a marine mammal medic for British Divers Marine Life Rescue (BDMLR). I assist the team with seal, porpoise, whale and dolphin rescues – primarily necessary as a result of human disturbance, watercraft noise and injury, or as bycatch by vessels fishing for other fish and ghost net entanglement.

- If you come across a seal on a beach, in a cove or on rocks it is so important to watch it from a safe distance so as not to cause it to panic.
- Seals regularly haul out on our coasts to digest their food and rest, but they can incur fatal injuries if they try to move too quickly on land to escape a threat such as an approaching human or dog.
- Please do not try to pull a stranded animal back into the sea as this can cause injury and they may need treatment or a period of recovery before they can swim strongly again.

Always leave a healthy seal alone unless you suspect entanglement, malnutrition, an abandoned pup or obvious injuries.

In such cases, call the 24-hour BDMLR rescue hotline immediately (01825 765546)

Please also call the hotline if you come across a live stranded whale, porpoise or dolphin, as it is not normal activity for them to beach themselves.

How can you . . . be a marine life volunteer?

With my newfound passion for rescuing larger marine life, my ocean journey led me to volunteer with my local Marine Conservation Group, the Mounts Bay

Marine Group, and the Cornwall Seal Group Research Trust. I have been able to assist these incredible groups with different projects in our area, such as the mapping, monitoring and restoring of our local seagrass beds, supporting marine plastic pollution projects, monitoring and identifying grey seals and even making short information videos for the G7 summit.

My sea swimming and snorkelling has become much more than a way for me to switch off and destress. It is a daily adventure driven by a goal to help preserve, protect and prolong the future health of our marine life and their entitlement to a safe and thriving home in the ocean.

AQUA ACTIVISM
FIGHT THEM ON THE BEACHES

What you get to know, often you grow to love and care for. One thing that can happen, as soon as you spend a lot of time in our waters, is that you come to care about their wellbeing as well as your own. You begin to notice signs of sewage, plastic waste and other pollution that not only impacts your safety and enjoyment as a swimmer, but may be affecting the health of the wildlife you swim alongside.

How can you...
become an activist?

Whether you're bothered about nurdles in the ocean, microplastics in our rivers or salmon farm pesticides in our seas, there's plenty you can do beyond moan about it – and countless campaigns and groups you can join.

As well as beach cleans and litter picks there are projects such as We Swim Wild which monitor microplastics. Or why not put your support behind a local campaign? Recent years have seen bids, across the UK, for designated bathing waters status – often those involved are as concerned about the ecological health of the places they swim as whether there are bugs there that make them sick.

How can you...
campaign for cleaner waters
and water monitoring?

Anyone who wild swims is probably aware of the frequent news stories around sewage discharges into our rivers from storm overflows or of agricultural spill-off into our waterways. Figures released by the Environment Agency in 2020 showed that just 14% of English rivers were of good ecological standard.

Concerns about how this might impact our health have spilled over into worry about the health of our waters as ecosystems. One way campaigners push for the monitoring and clean-up of these waters is to secure designated bathing water status for them.

What can you do...
to ensure water fit to bathe in?

In 2020, the River Wharfe at Ilkley became the first river stretch in the UK to be given designated bathing water status. On its first testing it was found to be 'poor quality'. As this book goes to print, applications are in place for such status to be given to Warleigh Weir on the River Avon and Port Meadow, a stretch of the Thames in Oxford. And so, citizen scientists from the Oxford Rivers Project have been collecting water from 18 river locations across Oxfordshire and sending them to Thames Water labs.

The point, for many of the campaigners, is not just to protect swimmers, but to draw attention to sewage entering the water and the impact that may be having on ecological systems. The rivers and waters we merely visit are home to other life.

To find out about the water quality in a particular area, receive alerts and report pollution or sickness from swimming, download the Surfer's Against Sewage Safer Seas & River Service app.

You might also like to get involved in campaigns around water quality by joining a local group, like London Waterkeeper, Cotswolds-based Windrush Against Sewage Pollution or Warleigh Weir Project Guardians.

SWIM-PICKINGS: CLEANING OUR SHORES

Most of us know what it's like to have the pleasure of a swim marred by stepping on a tangle of seaweed-entwined wet wipes or a plastic drink bottle floating past our nose. We could all sit back and whine, but it's far better to get involved in cleaning up.

LAURA TRUELOVE'S CLEAN-UP TIPS

A lot of people think that litter picking or beach cleaning is a waste of time because with every new tide brings new rubbish. However, every plastic ever created still exists and for every piece of plastic that you pick up on the beach there's one less piece of plastic in the marine environment. For me, that's why everyone should litter pick.

You don't have to go on a massive pick. Just keep some gloves and bags in your kitbag for whenever you go to the beach, whether you're swimming, going for a walk or surfing.

I really like the concept of Take Three for the Sea. Pick up three pieces of litter and be on your way. It's a really nice concept that shows you don't need to do a huge project, you don't need to be lugging big bags of rubbish from the beach. You can just take three things, dispose of them in an appropriate bin and feel good about what you did. If everyone did that we would have much cleaner beaches.

En masse – big beach cleans

While it's brilliant to do your individual beach clean, the great thing about getting involved in a mass beach clean is often they involve collecting data, a form of citizen science, as well as beach cleaning. This means you can feel your work might even have an impact on policy. To find out more about getting involved in mass beach cleans visit mcsuk.org or Surfers Against Sewage at sas.org.uk.

Campaign, volunteer, noise it up!

Five marine and river organisations and campaigns you can get involved with.

1 Marine Conservation Society

The UK's leading marine-environment conservation not-for-profit. Their goal is 'to recover the health of the ocean; for the sake of our wildlife, our climate and our own wellbeing'. Not only can you take part in their beach cleans, you can also get involved in educational activities with schools.

2 Great Nurdle Hunt

A project begun by the Scottish environmental charity Fidra, this has rolled out across the world. Now there is a yearly great global nurdle hunt. These tiny, persistent and potentially toxic plastic pellets are to be found in shocking quantities on many of our beaches, though frequently they can go unnoticed. But Fidra do more than encourage us to collect these pellets – they are also strongly pushing industry to change.

3 Surfers Against Sewage

Originally created in 1990 by a group of Cornish surfers, Surfers Against Sewage (SAS) is a marine conservation charity which works with communities to protect oceans, waves, beaches and marine life. You don't have to be a surfer to join, or fight sewage, or the plastic pollution that SAS is battling so hard against. You can simply be a swimmer or beach lover. Join one of their beach cleans or campaign for plastic-free communities. See sas.org.uk.

4 The Rivers Trust

Habitat creation, invasive species removal, river clean-ups – the Rivers Trust is where you go to volunteer for projects that get your feet wet. It's an umbrella organisation for 60 member trusts concerned with rivers in England, Wales, Northern Ireland and Ireland. With them, you can be part of reviving rivers to their former glory. See theriverstrust.org.

5 Sea Shepherd

Want to defend marine wildlife? Protect ecosystems? Stop illegal fishing? Clear the ocean of ghost nets? Established in 1977, Sea Shepherd's mission is to end the habitat destruction and slaughter of wildlife in the world's oceans. They are the controversial pirates of ocean activism. See seashepherd.org.uk.

THE BIG CHILL

THREE THINGS ABOUT COLD

Cold is the bliss and the bane of swimming outside the summer months. For some of us it's why we're there – the buzz that cold water shock can give us – for others it's something we endure because we love to swim in open waters, but there's no doubting that cold is an issue.

Bear in mind that, particularly on the west coast of England and Wales, the sea is at its warmest in the autumn, and even on a balmy hot day in April or May is likely to be only 12°C.

Lakes and waterfalls can be particularly chilly in winter, spring and even in early summer when snow and ice melt flows into them.

Generally we advise you to listen to your body and follow how you feel, rather than thermometer measurements and charts that tell you how long to stay in according to temperature – but also with an added warning of caution. Keep it short, especially if you're inexperienced.

Whether you wear a wetsuit or not is also up to you – do what makes you comfortable, and consider how long you want to be in the water. Bear in mind, too, that there are reasons other than cold for putting on the neoprene. We know plenty of swimmers who are all about the skins (bathing costume only) in the winter, but start wriggling their way into wetsuits when jellyfish season arrives.

1. COLD WATER SHOCK

Among the dangers of cold water swimming is the shock your body goes into the moment it is immersed in the cold.

'Even in summer months the water in the UK is cold,' says coach Sarah Wiseman. 'Cold water shock is caused by sudden immersion in cold water and can be triggered in water temperatures below 15°C. The sudden cooling of your skin can cause you to gasp involuntarily. Your breathing rate can change uncontrollably and significantly increase. These responses can contribute to feelings of panic and inhaling water into the lungs directly. This can happen quickly. Cold water shock can also increase the heart rate, and this can increase the chances of a heart attack. If you have any concerns do check with your GP before you take the plunge.'

Many people die following sudden cold-water immersion each year. Don't dive or jump suddenly into cold water, and if you do find yourself struggling with cold water shock, then please do follow the RNLI advice to float for around 60 to 90 seconds. This is the time it takes for the effects of the cold shock to pass and for you to regain control of your breathing.

2. AFTERDROP

Almost all of us swimmers have felt it. You get out of the water and you're feeling good – feels like you're stoked by a fire inside! – and then, before long, the cold hits and suddenly you're chilled, shivery, on the road, you fear, towards hypothermia. That's afterdrop: your body's continuing fall in temperature that goes on long after you've left the water. While you were in there your body constricted the blood vessels in your extremities, keeping warm blood in your vital organs, but once you're out of the water the vessels dilate, cooling the blood that runs through it and onwards to your core. Needless to say this can be extremely dangerous – and lead to hypothermia.

3. HYPOTHERMIA

Hypothermia is defined medically as a core body temperature of below 35°C. It creeps up on you gradually.

Hypothermia slows your thought processes down, so before you swim set your clothes out in the order you will put them on when you get out. Have your towel ready and at the top of the pile.

What to do if you are... experiencing hypothermia

- Get out of the water immediately.
- Don't rub your skin to dry – pat it.
- Remove ALL wet clothes as soon as you can and get changed into your dry set.
- Layer up in warm dry clothing including hat, gloves and warm socks.
- If possible find some shelter or somewhere warm.
- Stay out of the wind if it is windy.
- Drink something warm (not alcohol or caffeine) and eat some food.
- Do not use a shower or bath if you are experiencing hypothermia.
- Let your body shiver.
- Use a hot water bottle. Not directly next to the skin – wrap it up in a towel.

Last but not least, do not drive until you are certain it is safe to do so, or ask somebody else to drive you.

SARAH WISEMAN'S GUIDE TO THE SIGNS OF HYPOTHERMIA

Loss of coordination.

Changes in your swimming stroke – your body position may become more vertical in the water.

Arms and legs may feel heavy, numb, or sluggish.

Uncontrollable shivering and numbness in the body.

Clenched jaw and difficulty speaking.

Hands becoming claw-like and less ability to control them.

A feeling of elation and happiness.

WILD SWIMMING WITH KIDS

There's a whole other level of vigilance you need when you decide to take your kids on a cold-water swimming adventure. As well as questions of swimming ability, there's the issue of how long they can stay safely in the water – and chances are it's a lot less time than you. So, make sure you recognise the signs that they are getting cold (before they're blue-lipped and shivery), and get them hauled out of the water, wrapped up in plenty of towels, dressed and sipping on a hot chocolate, even if it feels like you're being a spoilsport and cutting short their fun. Bear in mind you might well have to help them get changed too – starting with persuading them to strip off those wetsuits and cossies. All this, most probably, while standing, dripping wet and getting colder yourself.

Selsey

STOKING THE FIRE INSIDE

The post swim warm-up is almost as much a part of the swimming experience as getting in the water itself, isn't it? Because getting warm is so important – so much so that one of the things we like to talk about most is how we do it, what we wear, what little tricks we have and, most crucially, what we put in our post-swim flask. Here's our guide to how best to get cosy after a chilling.

1 Tempting as it may be to hang around chatting – you're feeling that warm, happy buzz, why get dressed? – the most important thing to do is get your clothes on as soon as possible. Remember that afterdrop (see page 77) is real. Get out of those wet clothes before you find yourself shivering. Swim coach Sarah Wiseman advises 'start with the top half of your body'. This is where it's useful if you've left your clothes in a nice tidy pile (if it's sunny) in the order you'd like to find them when you're flailing for something warm, or neatly tucked in your bag (if it's raining or snowing), rather than strewn all over the beach asking for a drenching. Make sure, above all, that your towel is to hand.

2 Stand on a changing mat or bathmat – this stops your feet becoming colder.

3 A hot drink can be a big help in terms of warming up from the inside – whether it's hot Ribena, herbal tea or a tasty soup. What you really need to be paying attention to is your core body temperature, because it's still dropping as cold blood from your extremities is carried towards your organs.

4 Don't go straight from the cold into a hot shower – it can lead to collapse. As Dr Mark Harper puts it, 'If you have a really hot shower afterwards, that opens the blood vessels up to your skin and then all that cold from your periph-eries heads back into your core and makes it shockingly cold again.'

5 Pile on the layers. Insulated robes. Woolly hats. Fleecy bottoms. Even a charity shop fake fur coat. When it comes to keeping warm, part of the fun is the improvising and finding your own cosy kit.

6 We're great believers in moving around. Rather than drive home – or, worse still, sit in the car with the engine running – you're better off walking, cycling or even running. In fact, some of our favourite warm-ups have been the the craziest. An aerobics workout while singing 'Ride On Time' (without backing music)? A conga? A Haka-style stomp?

Annie Brooks likes to . . .
Lay everything out ready for when you get out the water, then you can focus on getting warm quickly. I like to sneak a hot water bottle onto my clothes to ensure I get super toasty. But to be honest, it's all about being fast in warming up. I used to get so sucked in by that post-swim high feeling that I'd forget about getting changed quickly, so speed is queen!

Laura Truelove recommends . . .
A dryrobe. I bought one last year and it changed my life. For ages, I was like, no I'm not getting one of them. Everyone's got one. I felt I wouldn't be a sturdy person who can put up with the winter, if I had one. Then I tried one and I thought, 'Oh, this is nice.'

Jonathan Cowie can't stop . . .
Dancing! Throwing some shapes is the best way to warm up.

Joanne Clement's top tip . . .
Walking and climbing is a great quick way to warm up. We love hiking to swim spots and clambering over rocks, and find we warm up very quickly after a swim this way.

SHIVERY BITES & HOT FLASKS

One of the things you learn quite quickly when you spend time with the wild swimming community is that no swim is quite complete without a shivery bite and a flask of some warming hot drink. What you put in your belly after the swim matters almost as much as the dip itself. It's your comfort. It's also, often, part of a social share.

Now, such snacks don't have to be cake – they can also involve a slap-up full breakfast in a café – but there are few cultures in which cake occupies such a central position as among wild swimmers. You have to be a real rebel swimmer not to eat your cake.

Clare Lord is a big fan of . . .

A flask of coffee and any homemade cake or scone, to be honest. I usually bake when I swim with friends and make pretty much anything that takes my fancy. This morning it was pink grapefruit and lime drizzle cake; last week I made raspberry and lemon scones.

Rhiannon Starks is all about the oats . . .

Ruth and I are massive fans of post swim porridge! We cook our porridge on our camping stoves and have been known to be creative with flavours. Ruth is more of a sweet porridge fan and her favourite is chocolate chip and chewy banana, while I like savoury porridge and recent favourites include dhal porridge and puttanesca porridge. We both agree that a hot chocolate, with oat milk, cardamom and date syrup is our favourite post swim potion.

Hannah Squire heats from within . . .

I love a hot chocolate in the winter with a banana (a surprisingly delicious combination), and in the summer a lovely cold apple juice and a few pieces of dark chocolate for energy and that wonderful bitter, chocolatey taste.

BISCOFF CAKE
... A PERFECT SWIM & SCOFF BAKE!

You will need
400g self-raising flour
260g caster sugar
2 teaspoons baking powder
180ml vegetable oil
400ml soya milk
Splash of vanilla essence
Splash of caramel flavouring (the flavoured coffee syrups are perfect!)

For the icing
1 tablespoon vegan marge
1 tablespoon Trex
Icing sugar
1 tablespoon Biscoff spread
1–2 tablespoons soya milk
A few Biscoff biscuits
Splash of caramel flavour

Method
1. Preheat your oven to 180°C and grease and line a couple of 7-inch cake tins.

2. Mix your flour, sugar and baking powder. Add the oil and soya milk and your vanilla essence and caramel flavouring. Barely mix, give the bowl a bash and pour into the cake tins. Bake for 25 minutes or until a skewer comes out clean.

3. Now make your middle icing by whisking together the marge, Trex and Biscoff spread, then adding your icing sugar to the desired consistency. You can use a little soya milk if it's too firm. Use this to sandwich the cakes together and then cool.

4. To make the top layer of icing, mix icing sugar, soya milk and caramel flavour to the desired consistency and spread on top. Crumble over some Biscoff biscuits and enjoy!

from Dips and Chips (see page 147)

Loughrigg

SKINS OR SUITS?

WHAT'S IN YOUR KITBAG?

JONATHAN COWIE,
Kendal
Editor, Outdoor Swimmer
JONNYHCOWIE

You don't need much to wild swim (for some a smile will suffice!), but a selection of useful kit will make your swim more enjoyable and safer.

1 **A tow float** will keep you safe by making you more visible in the water. Floats that double up as dry bags allow you to carry a small amount of kit, such as car keys, change of clothes, flip-flops and mobile phone in a waterproof case.

2 If you are winter dipping, a **bobble hat** will keep you warm. If you plan to put your head under, a colourful neoprene hat or two silicone hats is best for winter swimming. Whatever the season, always wear a bright hat to ensure you are visible to other water users.

3 A well-fitting **pair of goggles** is pretty much essential for swimming. Open water goggles are wider (so you can see more) with various lens options designed to cope with different weather conditions.

4 Protect yourself from **surfer's ear** – a condition in which the ear canal develops bony growths – by always wearing ear plugs, especially in cold water.

5 In cold water, a pair of **neoprene gloves** will keep your hands warm.

6 **Neoprene booties** keep your feet warm and offer some protection. Water shoes are also a good option to protect your feet from sharp stones and other hazards.

7 **Outfit options** include your birthday suit, trunks or cossie, or a wetsuit. If you choose to wear a wetsuit, do some research before buying as it will be the most expensive kit you purchase – from around £100 to more than £600.

8 **Different wetsuits** suit different styles of swimming. Wild swimming suits with neutral buoyancy and breaststroke wetsuits are available. For other swimmers, suits with buoyancy panels that correct body position when swimming freestyle could be a good option. For winter swimmers, there are thermal suits. Consider shortie, sleeveless and swimrun suits if you don't want head to toe neoprene. Made to measure suits are also available for a perfect fit.

9 **A changing mat** is useful – nothing is worse than trying to get dry and dressed while slipping about on a muddy riverbank. Use a doormat, bath mat, square of strong plastic or a cut-down yoga mat. Or use a large bag that you can stand in to get changed and then drop your wet kit into: options include bags for life and builder's rubble trugs. Rucksacks that fold out into mats are also available – get changed and then fold up the mat into a bag with all your wet kit inside.

10 **A changing robe** will allow you to get changed while preserving your modesty and will keep you warm and dry once you are dressed. A towelling robe is great for getting changed and dried under.

11 Having **the right kit to get warm** in afterwards is imperative. Loose layers (packed in your bag in the order you will put them on) are essential. In winter I wear a base layer, jumper, down jacket, fleece and a changing robe or a big coat. Wear loose, warm trousers that are easy to get into. And don't forget hat, gloves, thick socks, plus a flask of your favourite warm drink and a slice or two of cake!

Lake Windermere

OH, THE PLACES YOU'LL GO!

IN ENGLAND

Sweethope Lough

FENWICK RIDLEY,
Corbridge
Cold water coach & river trekker
📷 FENWICKRIDLEY

There's a real, deep connection you get from being in the water that a lot of us describe in different ways. It makes me feel re-energised. It is my happy place. I would happily live in a house in the water. Maybe I was a merman in a past life. I was a pool swimmer from a very young age and did my first mile in a pool at six years old. It was my escape from home because my mum was ill until I was sixteen.

I started open water swimming when I was nearly 21. After I did a big swim in the pool, 10 kilometres, my coach said, 'You need to do that in open water.' I was already swimming with my friends in the river, or the lake, but it had never really clicked for me before then to do mileage outdoors.

I now coach other people in open water. One of my biggest adventures has been swimming the North Tyne, walking and following the whole length of the river from Newcastle to Kielder, scaling it in seven days with a RuckRaft. It was an absolute beast, a real teacher of a challenge.

SWIM PATCH:
NORTHUMBERLAND

The countryside of Northumberland is stunning and blessed with the River Tyne, a lovely, dark, peaty river – but there are only a couple of sections I recommend, because the rest are quite hard to get to, or have an access or safety problem.

Tyne Green
📍 chosen.geese.ledge

Hexham's Tyne Green, which runs alongside the river, is a great spot to enter the North Tyne, and from there up until the first corner is a lovely stretch to swim along. There are a few things to be aware of, though. One is that it's quite an active stretch of the water – used by kayakers, SUP-boarders, rowers and fast-moving

River Tyne

vessels, with rowers sometimes taking up almost all of the river. This means it can be quite dangerous, particularly as you can find yourself swimming towards a rower who is going backwards. We constantly try to tell people that if you're going to swim there, stay river left (looking downstream) and always have a nice bright tow float.

Access to the water is really good: where the boat landing is and where the rowers get in and out, there's a lovely jetty with a nice slipway. It's shallow but there are a lot of rocks, so neoprene socks are useful. There are places on the stretch where there is agricultural spill-off, so ideally avoid days after heavy rain.

Sweethope Lough
◉ quietly.unite.slugs

This is the lovely lake venue where we run H2OTrails dip sessions of lifeguarded swims around a course. It's on private land and only accessible if you've booked through us. It's also so nicely tucked away and surrounded by trees that lots of people don't know it's there. People can book to join our sessions online at h2otrails.co.uk. The lake has a sand entry and you can stand up in 90% of the course, so it's perfect for beginners. We also run courses for kids.

This is a whisky barrel of a swim venue with a lovely peatiness. The water quality is unreal. It's the source of the beautiful River Wansbeck and also it's fed by a spring. Lots of people visit in the warmer seasons, but the venue is also perfect to help people get to grips with the idea of going down the temperature ladder. In winter, we run courses in cold water conditioning and preparation for ice swimming. Because it's so shallow and it's 240 metres up, it has a dramatic temperature fluctuation. Last year we had ice at the end of October. It's so brutal, lovely, and ideal for what we love to do.

> **SAFETY TIP**
> Attach a good whistle to your tow float.

Sweethope Lough

JANE BARNACLE,
North of Newcastle
🌐 BARNACLESWIMS

I live north of Newcastle, on the coast, with my partner David, who is also a keen swimmer, and our two dogs. My grandad loved sea swimming and swam every day well into his eighties. He took me and my sister swimming as children, so I've swum outdoors all my life. I swim every day in the sea but love river swimming most of all. I help run the Cullercoats OutDoor Swimmers (CODS).

SWIM PATCH:
THE NORTH EAST

We are very lucky in the north east of England to have a long sweep of amazing coastline. There are lots of beautiful beaches, from Tynemouth to Berwick (and beyond), and some wonderful rivers and lakes. We don't have as many visitors as some regions and there is still lots of space and many places feel unspoiled – though we are getting busier in the main tourist spots. There are outstanding places to see wildlife, such as at the Farne Islands or at St Mary's Lighthouse at Whitley Bay.

Tynemouth Longsands
📍 **stops.much.dunes**

Longsands is a long crescent bay near Newcastle, much loved by locals. The beach is backed by a pretty village and a historic priory. When calm, it's good for swimming, but it's also a renowned surfing beach and good for bodyboards and SUPs. The beach has a gentle, slow entry on beautiful golden sand. From there you can swim a mile or so along the shore or simply dip at the edge. A lively local swim group meets regularly.

Most people swim from the south end of the beach (locally known as Crusoe's, as that's where you will find a beach café, an excellent stop for post-swim refreshments), which is lifeguarded and there are public loos. Longsands can form rips, especially near a small stream at the south end, and in the middle of the beach, so swim north of that. It's always worth standing on the parking ramp to watch the sea, as the rips can usually be seen clearly from above.

On the far south of the beach is a disused outdoor pool and there is a local campaign to restore it (donate at tynemouthoutdoorpool.com), and on the beach there are two surf schools, offering small group sessions most of the year and also equipment hire. Parking is either on the ramp or further north on the road. It does get busy, is paid and the wardens are sharp.

River North Tyne, Chollerford
⚲ unfounded.mended.happier

In the heart of the Tyne Valley to the west of Newcastle, this is one of my favourite river swims. Combine a dip with seeing Chesters Roman Fort on the Roman Wall. The North Tyne is wild and peaty, a famous salmon river that rises near the Scottish border and flows through Kielder until

Tynemouth Longsands

it later meets the South Tyne at Warden Rock near Hexham to form the River Tyne. This part of the Tyne Valley is really rich in Roman history: forts at Chesters, nearby, and Vindolanda, only a 15-minute drive away.

Do check to see if there have been any releases from Kielder Reservoir (tyne-releasekielder.co.uk), as this will increase the flow. Park on the B6320 in a layby (warms.carefully.dispenser); get there early – it's popular. Entry can be gained from crossing the bridge to the opposite side of the George pub and walking down to the bank. Swim upstream against the current. The river gets deep fairly quickly and it's recommended to those who are confident outdoor swimmers only. It's particularly lovely in autumn when you can swim and admire the trees. I've seen kingfishers dart from the banks. Stop off after at the café at the Riverside Tearoom near the parking layby or at the National Trust Chesters Fort.

Beadnell Beach
◉ fuse.topped.trout

To the north of Northumberland, the beaches get wilder and less busy. Some are good for swimming and some less so. Beadnell is a lovely, very long crescent bay that has a harbour at the north end. On a clear day, the views towards Dunstanburgh Castle in the south are spectacular! It's a popular beach for kitesurfing on a windy day. The harbour is lively with boats and kayaks – look out for the historic lime kilns, too.

Park in the car park (farmer.absent.lakes), where there are also public toilets, but be early as Beadnell gets busy on a nice day. Most people swim from the harbour end of the beach. Keep an eye out for rips. Swimming is best at high tide or it's a very long walk to the sea! It's a deservedly popular beach, although there are no lifeguards, so be aware of other water users – boats, kayaks, SUPs and kitesurfers.

From the spring to late summer, the mid-section of the beach, known as 'Long Nanny' is roped off. This is a National Trust site which protects the nesting grounds of Arctic terns, little terns and ringed plover. There is a diversion from the beach to a viewing platform. This is a special place and it's important to keep dogs on a lead and observe the diversion.

There is a lovely café in the village, the Saltwater Café, plus a summer pop-up café in the beach car park, Bait.

ESSENTIAL KIT

An ancient merino vest has kept me warm for years.

BECCA HARVEY,
Sunderland
Searching for a quieter life
HARVMANIA

I first got into outdoor swimming through struggling with a PTSD diagnosis. I was desperate and, luckily, I saw a documentary about how swimming helped people with depression. I thought it was worth a punt. I knew there was a community nearby and tracked down a group who subsequently invited me for a swim. The group was focused around mindfulness and enjoying the water, and one January, in 4 degrees, I got in. As soon as I did, my pain melted away. I don't know whether it was a placebo effect or the temperature, but I was instantly addicted. It spurred me on through the darker times and gave me the resilience to keep pushing my abilities.

SWIM PATCH:
SUNDERLAND

I lived in the south for all my life and never considered coming to Sunderland until I met my partner, Michael, at the winter swimming world championships in Bled, Slovenia. Sunderland and the North east are quite honestly one big wonderful beach of variety, full of beautifully warm northern folk.

Roker Beach
sofa.sang.eagle

Roker was the first place I swam in Sunderland with Michael and it's a 15-minute drive from my house, so it's easy and has beautiful memories attached to it: wonderful bonfires on the beach, sleeping seals along the pier steps, Michael becoming entangled within the biggest lion's mane jellyfish I have ever seen...

The beach has two parts to it, but best is the section directly in front of the lifeboat station within the walls of the pier. You can swim on the other side, but I'm quite conscious of the rocks and the need to catch a good tide there, so I stick to what I know.

The beach within the pier is convenient, has ample parking nearby and constant local onlookers to give you that motivational boost. Sat at the end of the pier is a lighthouse, a beacon to watch as you spot your line in the water. The beach is predominantly sand but is covered in pebbles too.

If you want to venture further than the shoreline be aware that the River Wear meets the sea here and there can be strong currents. There's also an operational harbour, so be sure to wear a tow float if you're going towards the lighthouse. Apart from the safety aspects, this place is great for swimming. It has a real buzz and connection to the local community. There is an array of cafés and food outlets to choose from, whether you want cake, coffee or fish and chips to warm you up. It's a playground for distance, a beacon to push yourself, because even though you may be solo swimming you're still engulfed in the community here whether it's a Saturday morning or Wednesday afternoon.

Seaham Slope Beach
📍 **hometown.eased.offshore**

Where I live in Sunderland is right on the border of County Durham, so I also venture to Seaham for a swim. This is part of a working harbour, but has a car park that overlooks the beach. It's really handy to

Seaham Slope Beach

be able to grab a towel, go for a swim and then get back in your car to get changed. There are, however, only stairs to get down onto the beach, so access is an issue but a ramp is currently being discussed.

As it's part of a harbour, gated access to the beach and car park is controlled. If they believe the sea is too rough they will shut the gates and pop up a sign. It's best to check the usual weather and tidal apps beforehand as you want to reduce the chance of a wasted trip. It's also best to experience at high or incoming tide. Swimmers are advised to stay within the pier wall and the harbour wall known as 'the knuckle'.

The slope has a quaint black and white lighthouse that sits on the end of the pier protecting the beach from the force of the North Sea. There are usually people fishing along its wall, so don't be alarmed if you hear a bellowing hello from overhead during a swim. I personally love it down here in the dark, on a calm still night when the lights of the café on the corner illuminate the ripples. If you're lucky you'll also have an amphitheatre of vehicles lighting the beach for you on exit.

Seaham is at the heart of a collection of former coal-mining villages along the coast. You still have coal washing up on the beach most days at the slope, creating black waves and sand. It also leaves wonderful mountain-like pictures etched across the beach.

Roker Beach

POST SWIM WARM-UP TIP

Take two pairs of gloves with you in your kit. I was told this by Suzanna Cruickshank and it's a genuine life saver. Put one pair on as soon as you get out, don't even dry your hands, and then once you're dressed swap them out for a dry pair.

Lake Windermere

JAMES KIRBY AKA JUMPY JAMES,
South Lakes, Cumbria
Outdoor sports photographer & web developer
🌐 JUMPYJAMES.CO.UK

Swimming is a mindfulness adventure for me and makes me happy! The cold water dipping journey started for me on the 1st of January 2017, in a wintery Lake Windermere, inexperienced but willing to learn and challenge myself. Ice and snow have since become a major part of my winter adventures for photography and dipping. In summer I explore wilder places that aren't possible to reach with the limited daylight, unpredictable weather and riskier conditions of winter.

I suffer with noise-based anxiety and stress, so, for me, swimming is a purposefully mindful way to escape things for a while, to calm my mind and to enable me to become more mentally strong to the loud noises. As well as outdoor dipping, I swim indoors as well, to help with my technique and to get away from daily anxieties when I can't get to the wilder waters.

SWIM PATCH:
LAKE DISTRICT

A beautiful place, full of adventures that are all outdoors, in fresh air – and all sorts of water, rivers, tarns and lakes. The rain can be a huge issue for access to some places, owing to the rise and fall of the water levels; some weeks it feels like we are next to the sea! For me, it's the exploration of the landscape and seeing the scenery from the mountains which really makes me want to dip and swim here.

The whole of the Lake District becomes very busy in the summertime and it's very important to respect local access, to not park on grass verges and to understand that there may be fishermen and other water users in the same body of water.

Rydal Water, south side
📍 soonest.apple.hoofs

This is one of the smallest lakes in the Lake District, just over a kilometre long, and famous for its connections to William Wordsworth, who lived at Rydal Mount overlooking the water. You are in the land of the poets. I love to dip and swim here, as it's a beautiful place. There are a few places to swim from and the lake is dotted with tiny islands. There is wildlife, including otters, to watch if you are quiet, and places to explore. Toilets can be found in White Moss car park (nails.glare.ribcage). Head to the wonderful Badger Bar for a post swim meal, or an ale and a huddle up beside their log fire. Bins can be found at White Moss car park, the bus stop on the main road or in Ambleside.

Coniston Water, Monk Park
◉ **poetry.eggshell.squirts**

The views of Coniston Old Man are stunning and there's no better place to absorb them than while bobbing in the lake. Monk Park car park is at the lake's northern end and has a jetty to swim off, and it's a great place to start SUP-ing from. It's from here that many of the distance swims of Coniston start. Toilets and bins can be found in the car park.

Lake Windermere, Rayrigg Meadow
◉ **chickens.chef.snippets**

This is a beautiful place, in the largest natural lake in England, from which to watch the changing seasons. In springtime you can smell the wild garlic, in summer it's so green, and in winter you can dip or swim with a snow-capped mountain view! Park in the car park (where there are toilets and bins, plus a play area and picnic tables) and walk down to the jetty to enter the water. Several groups, including Mental Health Swims, swim from here.

Coniston

ESSENTIAL KIT

My camera, to take stunning photographs of where I've been, and my thermometer, to keep track of how cold my adventures are.

Coniston

JAKKI MOORE,
Millom & Haverigg
Artistic director of the Beggar's Theatre and Moore Arts: Millom
🌐 BEGGARSTHEATRE.COM

Swimming is my absolute sanctuary. I was brought up in Millom, by the sea, and we spent most of every summer holiday 'down the Rocks', the beach near to us. I learned to swim when I was about four, as my dad threw me in the 'pothole', and I loved it! I lived in Corfu for four years and I swam every single day in the sea, and scuba-dived. I began open water swimming in the Lakes when I was about 41 and took part in a few of the Great North Swim events.

Following the passing of my dad from lung cancer in 2016, I did a charity swim for Macmillan. I wanted to do 12 miles in 12 lakes in 12 days. But I actually swam 20 miles in 13 lakes in 12 days. It was awesome. I loved every minute!

SWIM PATCH:
SOUTH CUMBRIA

Coniston and Peel Island
📍 shepherdess.prospers.pats

A swim to the island made famous by *Swallows and Amazons* as Wild Cat Island. This is a perfect swim! The best entry point is on the east side of the lake by the jetty. It gets a little busy in high season and in 2020 was closed off, owing to the amount of visitors and dangerous parking. However, parking is often available at the Dodgson Wood car park. The swim across to the island is about 100 metres, or you can swim the whole width of the lake, about a mile, there and back, but watch out, the gondola does pass regularly in the summer season. I always swim with a tow float to be seen.

Coniston end to end is the furthest swim I've done. I am told it is just over five miles; however, my watch said 8.1 miles. Evidently, I'm not a straight swimmer! I tend to weave about as I get lost in my thoughts and let my body do the swimming.

Irish Sea, the Rocks, Hodbarrow
📍 wolf.reports.alternate

A great spot to swim off, but I also like to get in anywhere when walking along the beach from Haverigg to Silecroft. I don't actually swim far, although I dream of swimming to either Barrow across the water or the Isle of Man!

There can be lots of jellyfish on the beach and I often see them in the water. If the tide is out you really need to be careful as it comes in quickly and surrounds you. But the beach is just amazing, four miles long and, if the tide is out, it is just the most beautiful place to be: so quiet, too. You are in the shadow of Black Combe, as a famous poem by local poet Norman Nicholson goes.

Silecroft is now part of the coastal path and a new route has opened up which will take you further up the coast. They are building a new café on the beach, but for now you can pick up a coffee, ice cream or food from the Portakabin café. Toilets are available at Haverigg and Silecroft but nothing in between.

There is a naturist beach halfway, but I often don't see anyone. I tend to just get in in my underwear halfway along!

The Hollow, Hodbarrow Nature Reserve
◉ takers.restores.fires

A recent find for me. I began swimming in 'The Hollow', which was simply the sea until many years ago, when the sea wall fell, so they built a new one and now we have a massive lagoon where the water park is. In the evening when the sun is going down, it is so beautiful. I haven't ventured too far in there, as what is under the water is unknown. I did, however, swim my first time in the top end of this lagoon before my first Great North Swim.

The best time to go is in the evening. You look around and it is just stunning. Lighthouses are all along the sea wall, the beach is there, you are again in the shadow of Black Combe, and the distant fells and mountains are amazing. Be aware, though, that there are no amenities.

Essential kit
Tow float and mobile phone case. I always have to take pics in the water!

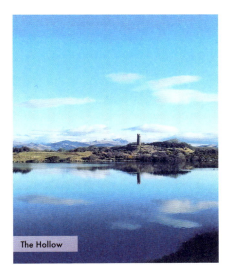
The Hollow

CLARE LORD,
The Fylde Coast
Chartered legal executive
📍 BAYMOPS

I have always loved the outdoors and been a bit of a water baby, as I was brought up sailing with my parents. Because of a number of surgeries to my leg I can no longer run or climb the fells so I was looking for a hobby that took me outdoors but was less impactful on my body. In April 2017 my friend suggested swimming at a local water park and within minutes of me getting in I knew I was hooked. I set off on my outdoor swimming journey in a wetsuit, but for the past two years I have swum skins all year round.

SWIM PATCH:
LANCASHIRE

I divide my life between Lancashire and Wales; from my house in Prestatyn I can walk to the sea in two minutes. I'm also only about an hour's drive from Snowdonia National Park, which offers similar swimming options to the Lake District – llyns, small llyns and rivers.

Mary's Shell
📍 melon.ferried.ledge

Mary's Shell is a sculpture that has been located in the tidal area of the sea at Cleveleys and forms part of the Mythic Coast Art Trail. It is huge and when the tide comes in you get some pretty cool photos of it partly submerged. It is in the popular seaside town of Cleveleys, which is north of Blackpool. There is lots of parking, and access into the water is from the promenade and down the steps. Again, you need to keep an eye on the tides, as this area is tidal. This part of the coast isn't sheltered and it can be very wavy and exciting, but when it is calm it's all the better for exploring the shell.

Morecambe Bay
📍 sticky.stove.hurls

Affectionately known by local swimmers as 'Mallows Bay', as most people start swimming there after joining MALLOWS (the Morecambe and Lancaster Lancashire Open Water Swimmers) Facebook group.

Mary's Shell

Just east of the Stone Jetty, this perfectly formed bay is overlooked by a large clock tower and the Eric Morecambe statue. Nearby there is a memorial to Commander Charles Gerald Fosberg OBE RN, who was a Master Mariner in the Second World War and a marathon swimmer who held the English Channel world record in 1957.

The bay has plenty of parking close by, toilets and an RNLI station. It is very tidal, which means you can't swim there on every tide. If the high tide is less than seven metres then you should avoid swimming there as you will need to wade out to get into water that is deep enough to swim. This is not recommended as the sandy beach turns into mud flats where you could get stuck and there are strong tidal currents at the mouth of the bay that should be avoided at all costs.

Provided you enter the water only on a tide over seven metres, there is ample opportunity to swim within the confines of the bay parallel to shore. Because the bay shelves very gradually you don't get 'dumping waves' and so can easily enter through gentle breakers and find yourself in a lovely big swell you can bob around in.

CERI OAKES,
Whitby
Photographer
📷 WHITBY_WILD_SWIMMERS

As a photographer I am drawn to the sea because it fascinates me how it is so changeable; it can be equally as beautiful when it is as still as glass, reflecting the pink glow of a sunset, as it is under an angry grey sky with rolling waves attacking the sea wall. Discovering that I could get even more joy from being in the sea was a wonderful revelation and led to me starting up the Whitby Wild Swimmers.

SWIM PATCH:
WHITBY

Whitby is unusual in that, despite being on the east coast, it faces north – so at certain times of year you can watch the sun both rise and set over the water.

Whitby Beach
📍 radiated.visitors.custard

This long, sandy beach has a view of the town's protective piers to the south and the rugged cliff at Sandsend village to the north. Whitby and the Gothic abbey ruins inspired Bram Stoker to write *Dracula,* and if you swim close to the piers you can see St Mary's Church and the old weather-beaten graves on the clifftop.

Be careful at high tide to note your exit and entry points, as the water reaches the sea wall and cliffs with only a few areas safe to get in and out. Be careful, too, of rip currents. We have been joined on our swims by seals and dolphins in the summer months. Our favourite places to

Sandsend

get in are the slipway beside the West Pier or in front of Whitby Surf School, an area which is lifeguarded in the summer.

There are public toilets nearby and at Whitby. If you make the trek back up the 'zigzag' paths it is worth stopping at Clara's for a hot drink and to sit and watch the sunset.

Sandsend
📍 dragonfly.improving.confident

The same stretch of beach but two miles north of Whitby, this village is a beautiful picture-postcard scene with some great little cafés for enjoying a post-swim cake and hot drink. If you are an experienced long distance swimmer you can swim from Whitby to Sandsend or vice versa, depending on the tides. We usually enter the water just in front of Sandside café. It is perfect here, because even at high tide there is always some beach to get in and out onto. We've had post-swim campfires here and enjoyed a moonlit swim on a full moon. If you're new to swimming at Sandsend, it is a good idea to familiarise yourself with the beach at low tide as there are rocks and wooden groynes that become hidden as the tide comes in.

LES PEEBLES,
Giggleswick
Wild swim tour guide
THEDALESDIPPER

About three years ago I was working on a decorating job in the Lake District in the village of Grasmere, and each day I was driving past the beautiful lake there. It was twinkling in the sunshine, and it just kept catching my eye, and I thought, 'On my last day I'm going to bring my swimming trunks and I'm going to get in there.' And that's what I did. Little did I realise how much that one swim would kind of change for me. While I was in one sense perfectly happy, I didn't quite have my mojo. But I got in the water, and my mojo was returned.

When I came home, I met some other people who swam and we set up the Dales Dippers group and soon I became a swim guide and started to get paid for what I love doing.

SWIM PATCH:
YORKSHIRE DALES NATIONAL PARK

This national park is an area of outstanding natural, rugged beauty with some of the best waterfalls and river swimming and dipping in the UK. As well as Hardraw Force, the biggest single-drop waterfall in England, I would recommend both Stainforth Force and the Eel Pool. I class them as two different dips, because one, Eel Pool, is a river swim and the other, Stainforth Force, is a waterfall, even though they are close to each other in the River Ribble.

Eel Pool, River Ribble
polite.slept.enjoy

Though this is a well-known spot, a bucket-list swim for many, always busy during the hot days or bank holiday weekends, go outside those times and you can sometimes have it to yourself. It's about 60 metres of long, swimmable river, 10 to 12 feet deep, very dark and peaty-looking, depending on the weather. Sometimes it may even look black. Here, you sit on the edge and launch in rather than go in gradually. It's where I do all my introduction sessions with newbies, and they're totally blown away with it, as are most people,

Eel Pool

because it's such a beautiful stretch.

With all of these spots, I recommend checking the weather beforehand and I'm always checking, with my goggles, under the water as well, especially after rain, because over the years I've seen the river move the most amazing amount of stuff. We've had whole trees delivered to the Eel Pool, and then a week later picked up again and taken somewhere else.

Parking is at the local village of Stainforth, where there is a pay and display National Parks car park. From there, it's a seven or eight minute walk down to the river. Access is from a footpath that runs alongside the campsite side of the river.

The Eel Pool is reached by a gravelly muddy path that's not suitable for people with any type of limited ability or balance issues. I recommend walking boots and also suggest to my newbies that they bring walking poles if they've got any balance issues at all.

Stainforth Force
◉ dice.rehearsal.scrolled

This is a triple fall waterfall, and not safe to swim in when it's in spate, as is the case for most of the places in the Dales.

Stainforth Force can be very, very dangerous at such times. But it's a phenomenal sight.

At other times it is a delight to swim in. Park at Stainforth village (handlebar.bins.seaside) and access via the footpath that runs along the campsite side of the river. The Force is fairly easy to get into in the right conditions. One of the dangers around both this and Eel Pool is that the rock in the local area is limestone. When it gets wet, it's like an ice rink and very easy to fall over on.

I always encourage people simply to sit and have a cup of tea for five minutes before they get in. That's what I do, because, while I've swum in these places hundreds of times, I've never been in the same water twice, so it just gives me an opportunity to have a look and make sure it's as I'm expecting it to be.

The riverbank where the path runs is owned by Knight's Stainforth campsite, which runs a bar, café and restaurant called the Knight's Table. Great food, great drink, great beer, great prices, great services, indoor and outdoor seating!

Hardraw Force
📍 **hurray.momentous.decorated**

England's highest single-drop waterfall plunges a hundred feet and is mind-blowing in terms of its scale. You need to pay to visit – at the moment, adults are £4

> **SAFETY TIP**
>
> We've got a saying in the Dales: 'If in doubt, stay out.'

and children £2.50 – but there is a café, toilets, visitor centre and nice path all the way in. It used to be owned by the pub next door, but a few years ago it was bought by a private individual. There is parking, either right next to the tourist centre, where there's room for about twenty cars or you can park out on the road.

A 5-minute walk takes you up to the waterfall, and there are marked walks you can do around the grounds as well. Given that it's a tourist attraction, you're always guaranteed an audience! More often than not when I get in, people who haven't planned to swim, strip off and join me. It is a breathtaking waterfall and a lovely pool where you can get plenty out of your depth. The key safety tip is: don't ever get in right under the waterfall, whatever the conditions might be. I've done that once when it was very light, and it was extremely sore. Also go see Hardraw when it's in spate – it's breathtaking. There's no way you would get in then, but it's worth going just to have a look.

Hardraw Force

Withens Clough

NIC WILKINSON,
Mytholmroyd
Primary school teacher
WILD_SWIMMING_CALDERVALLEY

I began wild swimming in spring 2020 and I cannot emphasise how much it has changed my life! After that first time, I was instantly hooked. I had finally found something that I had needed that was just for me, something that helped me to reset and something that made me feel incredibly proud of myself. Every time I plunged into cold water, I felt a sense of stress and tension leave my body and my mind. At the beginning of 2021, I started a wild swimming Instagram page to share my experiences and I recently started a weekly swim group. It is so lovely to have a post-swim brew and natter with other people who are becoming just as hooked on wild swimming as I am!

SWIM PATCH:
YORKSHIRE

Some of my favourite swims are in reservoirs. However, byelaws prohibit swimming in some Yorkshire Water reservoirs. See Owen Hayman (page 39) for more on the legality of swimming in reservoirs and the campaigns for greater access, as well as safety information.

Ryburn Reservoir
📍 **heads.beauty.losses**

This reservoir feels special to me because it's where my children love to have a picnic and watch me swim, plus it's the place where I held my first-ever wild swim group and people actually turned up! Buses 587 and 901 stop close to the reservoir. Arrive following a beautiful 10-minute walk through the woods to get in at an easy entry point complete with a bench and plenty of trees for privacy.

It's possible to combine a swim at Ryburn with another, a short walk away, at Baitings, where the big thrill is that there you can swim under a bridge – incredible!

Withens Clough
📍 **returns.easels.elders**

A reservoir with spectacular views, fields and trees for miles, as well as a local landmark, the Stoodley Pike monument. Parking is free and available at a car park on Withens New Road. Best entry point is at the three words given, as it is quite unexpectedly sandy and very shallow to begin with and gradually becomes deeper. I love how vast the water is here, how I feel so small in such a huge body of water and how wild it feels to be completely surrounded by nothing but raw nature. The weather can change in an instant. It goes from still and calm to windy and dramatic within minutes.

For refreshments after your swim, head to the Blue Teapot café in Mytholmroyd for gorgeous coffee and cake, or there's a lovely bar called Barbary's in Mytholmroyd where we sometimes go for a post-swim glass of wine or beer after a teatime sunset dip!

North Bay, Scarborough
📍 mats.poetic.worth

A long expanse of sand, stretching from the Sea Life Centre to Scarborough Castle, with a promenade along its length. There's nothing quite like a swim in the sea here; it's simply breathtaking. The long waves breaking towards the castle end also make it a surf destination. When I visit Scarborough, I tend to book a beach chalet for the day for a real treat. My fondest memory was in May 2021 – having a dip in the morning when we first arrived and then another dip just as the sun was setting. Just, wow! Sitting in the beach hut warming up after my sunset dip, with a cup of tea and a bag of chips (plenty of salt and vinegar, of course) looking at the sea I had just been in was truly beautiful. I savoured every last second.

ESSENTIAL KIT

My Swim Feral changing bag has been a game-changer. I can stand inside my bag while getting changed, keeping the cold off my feet and the wind off my legs, and it has compartments for all of my bits and pieces. They're handmade in Yorkshire from recycled materials.

JAMIMA LATIMER,
West Yorkshire
Artist, founder of Swim Feral and creator of the Turtleback bag
🐢 SWIMFERAL

When I discovered outdoor swimming, I was in the throes of an early menopause and having long bouts of chronic insomnia. I'm a really active person but was often too exhausted for regular exercise. Swimming, however, I could do. I found the water gave me back the energy I'd lost. Swimming calmed everything, it reset my body and mind. It's helped me deal with everything life has thrown up. It's a daily ritual for me now. It was, and still is, the best therapy I've ever had.

SWIM PATCH:
CALDER VALLEY

Todmorden and Hebden Bridge are quirky, vibrant small towns nestled in the Calder Valley. Walk up a hill in any direction and you will find yourself in awe-inspiring open countryside. There are plenty of small dipping places, but Gaddings Dam tops them all.

Gaddings Dam, Todmorden
📍 jiffy.skills.exotic

A friend described Gaddings as a 'Thin Place'; this Celtic term means a portal between worlds, places where other dimensions seem closer. This is how it feels for me.

High up on the Yorkshire moors, exposed to the elements and with panoramic views, reached by a significant hike up a steep hill, this landscape has the ability to make you feel very small and put the world into perspective. Some days it can feel like swimming in liquid silver, with the clouds reflecting in the water and the next day be as steely, mean and fierce as the North Sea – it holds all the emotions.

Gaddings is an earth embankment dam located on top of the moors between Todmorden and Walsden. Constructed in 1833 to supply water to the mills of Lumbutts, the reservoir fell into disuse when the mills began to use steam power. Slated to be drained in 2001 owing to its poor condition, the reservoir was rescued by a determined group of locals

Gaddings Dam

who bought the dam, repaired it, and now continue to maintain it. Please consider becoming a friend of Gaddings Dam; your £10 a year will help pay for its upkeep.

Much has been made of the dam having the highest beach in the country. It does have a very small sandy beach in one corner, which attracts a lot of day trippers laden with inflatables and windbreaks in the hot weather, but people are often disappointed after the long sweaty hike up the hill that the beach is way smaller than expected.

There's an unofficial well-worn path straight up the hill, but the landscape is corroding from overuse, so it's better and safer to use the slightly longer marked stone path which is clearly signposted. Limited parking is available on Lumbutts Road by the Shepherds Rest Inn (prone. shave.apparatus), but there have been problems with inconsiderate parking during busy times making it impossible for emergency services to access, so it's better to park in Todmorden and walk up. An extra 20 minutes, but a beautiful walk.

ESSENTIAL KIT

A Turtleback bag, of course – it's an insulated changing mat and a bag all in one.

OWEN HAYMAN,
Sheffield
Horticulturist & Outdoor Swimming Society inland access officer
OWAINHAEMAN

I grew up on the coast in Swansea, loving the sea and experimenting with winter dipping before it was 'a thing'. When I was 19 I moved to Sheffield for university where I discovered so much open water, but almost nowhere to swim because it was all reservoirs and you weren't allowed in them. After a few years I became part of a Leeds Facebook group that was swimming in many reservoirs, some close to Sheffield. One day I joined them for a swim, and pretty soon I had set up a similar group, SOUP – Sheffield OUtdoor Plungers, where I started building a swimming community and, along with others, sharing my swims in the many active and disused reservoirs that span from the city centre out into the Peak District. Since 2016, the group took Sheffield from a place with a tiny handful of swim spots to being seen as one of the best inland cities for outdoor swimming, provided you are happy to trespass respectfully.

SWIM PATCH:
SHEFFIELD

Sheffield is a magical city for many reasons. It has a rich industrial heritage that lives on today not just in modern industry but in music, architecture and the surrounding landscape. The Peak District boundary hugs the west of the city. A spider's web of river valleys, woods and moors permeate the urban boundary, where a big handful of reservoirs are within easy travelling distance of much of the city.

Only three years ago, it was still a surprising and sometimes shocking thing to see swimmers in reservoirs in the area. In the past few years, things have really turned around and the general public seems to be coming around to the idea that reservoirs are not necessarily swirling whirlpools of pipes and machinery, but hugely undervalued blue spaces.

For more on reservoirs, see page 39. For a guide to access, see page 65.

Crookes Valley Park
◉ glass.loving.moons

A fairly small park just outside the city centre, with a bowling green, fabulous cherry trees, wildflower meadow areas and a large clear-water lake once used for boating. The lake is a disused reservoir built in the 1780s, historically known as the Old Great Dam, with its own pub just next to it, the Dam House. For decades people have said it is 60 feet (18 metres) deep, but scuba explorations tell us it is actually a much less intimidating eight metres in the middle. The park is in a student area of the city, right next to Sheffield University. Ponderosa Park and Western Park sit beside it, both lovely. There are excellent public transport links to the park, via bus or a short walk from the tram, as well as various free and paid parking nearby.

The most popular entry point is from the 'jetty' in front of the pub, but you can get in anywhere you fancy. Stay away from the shallow corner with the little island – this is the wildlife corner and is vital for nesting birds and fish spawning. It's waist-deep from the get-go, and fairly quickly you're out of depth. The water ranges from crystal clear in winter and spring, becoming a little green and cloudy in summer.

The lake is open for free fishing, so we are careful to maintain a good relationship with the fisherfolk. Give them a wide berth, but be polite and say hello. Be aware that Sheffield City Council do not permit swimming in the lake, but are not actively trying to prevent it. No byelaws are stated at the site.

Broomhead Reservoir
◉ after.waking.custard

A large and fairly sheltered reservoir in a quieter area of the Peak District, a valley full of woodland, coppices, nature reserves and old quarries on the hilltop. A good network of footpaths allows you to

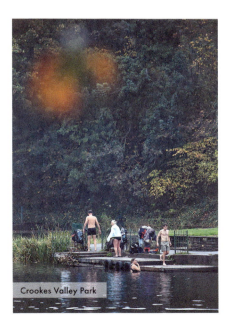
Crookes Valley Park

Broomhead Reservoir

explore it all. The woods at the western end of the reservoir have an unusually high abundance of copper beech.

The water is the colour of black tea or cola, due to dissolved organic carbon that percolates from the peat bogs up on the moors. The reservoir shore is dense with gnarly willow tree 'mangrove'. When water levels are lower, a stony, sandy beach is exposed around the reservoir. At low water levels, entry is easy all around, but especially at the big beach that becomes exposed at the western end, furthest from the dam wall. This beach has a very gradual slope into the water when walking straight towards the dam wall at the far end, making it great for beginners. However, there is a sudden drop towards the right to be aware of. There are also entry points on both the north and south shores. There are designated parking areas at various points around the reservoir.

Please be aware that Yorkshire Water does not permit swimming at this site.

Waterswallows Quarry
marsh.absorbs.bless

Waterswallows is a disused flooded basalt quarry, a very inert volcanic rock. The basalt is around 320 million years old, making the quarry a site of special scientific interest, owing to the interesting geological exposure. The quarry is just down the road from where Buxton mineral water is bottled, which makes sense when you see the crystal clear water.

The quarry does have an industrial feel, which means its beauty is sometimes an acquired taste. Rich wildflower communities thrive on the poor rocky soils. The whole south and western side of the Peak District is characterised by the quarries and train lines that serve them. Many of these are now disused, leaving ample adventurous swimming opportunities.

The old train lines are often repurposed to provide gentle and scenic off-road cycle routes, such as the Tissington Trail, High Peak Trail and the Monsal Trail.

There are various water entry points at Waterswallows, but the easiest one is where a zigzag roadway enters the water on the lake's east side. Access this by walking from Daisymere Lane (on the west side) around the southern end of the lake, where you will see the obvious water entry point. This has a gradual entry, stony underfoot. The site is popular with locals and scuba divers too.

Buses stop on the A6 nearby and you can park on Daisymere Lane. Access to the quarry is by trespass only. But if you choose to do this, the gate can be stepped over, and gaps found in the fence. Unlike some quarries there is little to stop you entering the site.

SWIM TIP

A bit controversial, but don't be afraid to go alone. Simply match the added risk of being alone by being extra cautious with what you do. Being with other people can give you a false sense of security. We swim at our own risk, and to me that means not depending on other people for my safety. In a group of people I definitely tend to go further and stay in longer than if I were alone, and I've seen the consequences of that.

RUTH SLATER,
Derbyshire & the Peak District
Educational psychologist
CAMPBELLBLACKBOARD

I have swum outdoors in rivers, lakes, tarns and the sea all my life. About five years ago I noticed the significant positive impact it had on my mental health and began swimming in wild places most days, all year round. I was first diagnosed with acute clinical depression more than forty years ago and, without doubt, plunging into icy water is, for me, the most immediate way of getting rid of even the worst symptoms. I used to swim alone, or with willing friends (usually bribed with the promise of a picnic). However, about three years ago I discovered social media and, most significantly, the Sheffield Outdoor Plunger Facebook group, and my life has been transformed.

SWIM PATCH:
DERBYSHIRE & THE PEAK DISTRICT

These regions offer a huge variety of swim spots, from moorland pools to waterfalls and reservoirs, with the magnificent River Derwent and its tributaries running through stunning countryside. There is so much to explore. Wandering up a stream onto the Kinder Plateau or walking along river valleys can reveal hidden gems of dipping spots. Map-reading skills and an understanding of rivers really help, but if you are not confident there are several well-known spots (highlighted here and on the SOUP Facebook page). There are also some of the most welcoming wild swimmers, who will meet for swims should you ask.

Chatsworth
📍 **tidal.builds.reddish**

Park at Calton Lees car park and wander across the cattle grid and down to the River Derwent. The best swimming is between the two weirs, and muddy entrance points can be spotted at both ends of this stretch. Even on the busiest of summer days, when families and groups of youngsters congregate around the bottom weir to picnic and plunge, you can quickly find solitude by swimming slowly upstream. The surroundings of Chatsworth are simply magnificent, and the house reflected in still waters is a sight for sore eyes. In the winter, it is moody and mysterious. In the autumn you will often hear, and sometimes see, the rutting and calling of the stags.

Early mornings are the best for wildlife, with deer and lambs creeping right up to the water, oblivious to quiet swimmers. Kingfishers, mandarin ducks, cormorants, geese, wagtails all frequent this beautiful stretch. And from spring to summer, sand martins can be seen darting and diving over your head in their hunt for tasty treats. If you are lucky, you may even see them speeding into their holes in the sandy riverbanks.

Whatever the season, whatever the weather, whatever the time of day, Chatsworth has the power to take my breath away. I have been enjoying these magical waters for the past fifty years, and they have never failed to heal, calm and bring joy.

Three Shires Head
📍 **yummy.eagles.jaws**

Remote, wild and stunningly picturesque, this was one of my favourite paddling destinations as a child. There are numerous

Slippery Stones

pools which are deep enough to swim in, so bring a picnic and take your time to explore. This beauty spot can be very busy, so either avoid at the weekend, or visit early or later in the day. Any journey here will need to be planned carefully (with respect to the rural communities in the area) and there is no closest or best approach. Parking is limited. It can be approached from Flash village, Wildbourclough and Gradbach along good footpaths and bridleways. My favourite route heads over the moors and drops down to this heavenly oasis, often with the haunting cries of moorland birds in the background.

Three Shires Head

Slippery Stones
♦ magical.bedspread.drags

High in the Derwent Valley, above the awesome Ladybower and Howden reservoirs, is a fabulous plunge pool. The walk (or bike ride) into this pool is straightforward; at the weekend you can park at the very end of the single-track road (Kings Tree) turning point and follow the track into the wilderness. When you reach the footbridge (where it is also possible to dip), turn left away from the circular cycle route, and the plunge pool is a short way upstream. It has a magnificent and remote feel but is perfect for a dip or a picnic. I tend to double dip, with a wild romp onto Bleaklow or Margery Hill in between swims. It is also a brilliant stopping-off point of the circular cycle route around the reservoirs (all well worth a trip). Again, this spot does get busy on warm days. However, go early, late or in the winter months (my favourite!) and you are likely to have it all to yourself.

WARM UP TIP

Walk uphill fast.

Chatsworth

JADE HANLEY,
Manchester
Creator of the Wild Swim podcast
🌐 WILDSWIMPODCAST.COM

I swim at least weekly in and around Manchester. My once-in-a lifetime swim experiences include swimming from the Golden Gate Bridge to Alcatraz, swimming in 0.9°C water in Iceland and swimming under a rainbow.

SWIM PATCH:
MANCHESTER

Greater Manchester isn't top of people's wild swimming lists, but actually there are several convenient locations not far from the city. Swimming in Salford Quays feels so urban, with the high-rise apartments and offices. I love a swim in an idyllic location, but there's something special about doing laps while watched by bemused Man Utd fans on their way to a game. Also nearby is Sale Water Park, a manmade lake south of the city centre. A swim at these venues must be part of an organised session: there is a small fee to pay, and swimming outside these times is banned.

OpenSwim, Sale Water Park
📍 stone.each.cycles

Sale Water Park's origins are inauspicious – it was dug out to raise the level of the nearby M6 – but it does feel much 'wilder' than the location might suggest. Trees line the banks and a circular path runs around the lake itself.

Swimming at the organised sessions takes place in a marked area with different courses on offer. Safety cover is provided and coaching is available. There are swimruns and night swims. But the best swimming at Sale is in the morning of a beautiful sunrise. In shallower parts of the lake it's possible to admire the catfish that call the lake home. Oh, and if anyone finds the camera I dropped in the water a few years ago, I'd love it back!

Salford Watersports Centre & Uswim!, Salford Quays
📍 upset.just.muddy
📍 scenes.lovely.thank

Queen Victoria opened Salford Docks in 1894, and it was once the third busiest port in Britain, before closing in the 1980s. Like a lot of post-industrial sites, the area became derelict before being transformed through regeneration, with the introduction of the Lowry theatre, the Imperial War Museum North, and the BBC and ITV.

These two venues are in neighbouring docks and offer organised sessions on alternating days. Although it's in an urban setting, the water quality is very good. Swimming takes place around marked courses of various distances, sometimes spanning the full length of the docks (up to 500 metres at Salford Watersports and 1 kilometre at Uswim!). Both venues offer events, such as the Neon Night Swim and Greater Manchester Swim at Uswim!, and the Halloween Swim at Salford Watersports. I've found the staff really friendly, happy to assist whether you're new or looking for advice on training.

A personal favourite is swimming under the big red footbridge at Uswim!, trying to imagine you're in San Francisco. In spring and autumn you can swim under a spectacular sunset, if the legendary Manchester rain holds off.

Kit tip

Only take clothes you can put on with numb fingers.

Salford Watersports

BETH & HANNAH SQUIRE,
Shropshire
Photographer (Beth)
Curator, historian & writer (Hannah)
BEASQUIRE & HANNAH_SQUIRE

Our favourite time to swim is in the winter, when the water feels warmer than the air. Having both loved swimming and being outside in nature since we were kids, in September 2020, with pools closed and the stay-at-home order in full effect, we realised we needed to be a bit more adventurous if we wanted to find places locally to swim. I, Hannah, suffer from mental health issues of anxiety and depression, both of which were heightened during lockdowns, so I found swimming a great escape, the perfect form of watery meditation. You can't be anything but present and in your body when you are wild swimming.

SWIM PATCH:
SHROPSHIRE

Shropshire is one of England's least populated counties and there are some amazing, quiet spots to swim, most of which require some walking, and mean you get away from the noises of modern life – the cars, phones and houses – and feel fully embraced in nature.

Carding Mill Valley Reservoir
📍 winks.overheard.hungry

This reservoir is believed to hold 12 million gallons and was built after the decline of the local wool industry to support Church Stretton's aspirations of becoming a health resort and spa location. Owing to its depth, the water always feels still, calm and refreshingly cold. It's so dark, it seems mysterious, and we often joke about what monster could be lurking in its depths!

This hilltop spot is incredibly peaceful, a manmade reservoir cocooned by trees on three sides, and with a fourth that has amazing views across Shropshire's heather-covered hills. The wind through the trees makes a beautiful sound; the only other noises are the occasional bleating of sheep coming to quizzically stare at you while swimming, or the pop of fishes coming up to gollop up flies resting on the water's surface.

River Teme, Ludlow

This is a National Trust site and there's a lovely café for after-swim refreshments (the cakes include gluten-free and vegan options), and clean, modern toilet facilities. It's a scenic 10-minute walk from the top car park, meandering on the way past two smaller mill ponds, often surrounded by sheep and wild Welsh ponies.

A manmade stone beach area offers a gradual entry to the water and the perfect place to sit and rest, still partially submerged. The lovely old industrial tower which sits in the middle of the water is a great place to swim to and around – but should not be used for diving or jumping off, because of its age and height.

Boyne Water, Brown Clee
📍 uptown.patrolled.stopwatch

It takes 25 minutes from where we park near Ditton Priors village to walk to this lake, but the anticipation and the views across the hills are part of the fun.

A manmade lake, with steps down into the water, this is so fully surrounded by reeds and embraced by the landscape one would be forgiven for imagining it has always been here, part of nature's design. It's secluded, encircled by trees, far from the road and nearby Ditton Priors, but with views across the local heather-covered landscape. An escape from the modern world, you can't help but feel as if you're the only people to have discovered it. The tranquillity of the spot and the calmness of the water are my favourite aspects. Plus, it's so full of peat we always marvel how orange our limbs look in the water.

The Willows café in Ditton Priors has a wonderful garden to sit and enjoy a lovely cooked breakfast, with great views over the countryside, after a long swim.

River Teme, Ludlow
📍 disposal.mandolin.lied

A great place for spotting curious swans with their cygnets and lots of other wildlife, both in the water and on the river banks, this is a gorgeous wide river, not too fast-paced most of the year. Perfect for exploring and seeing historic Ludlow and the countryside from a different angle. We love swimming the twists and turns of the river, listening to the sounds of the moving water and of the local wildlife.

The best place to enter the water is the Linney Riverside Park, either at the canoe landing stage, opposite the car park, or slightly further downriver at a quieter, more secluded entrance. From there, swim towards the gorgeous Dinham Bridge for more wonderful views. It can get busy in the summer, so look out for other swimmers and canoeists! (Toilets, picnic benches and a play area are in the park.)

Opposite the bridge and a short walk from the car park is the Green Café (housed in the old mill building), which serves delicious vegan burgers and hot chocolates, perfect for after a swim. It has a hydro-electric waterwheel, which still generates power for the building.

> **WARM UP TIP**
>
> Hannah: I love to go for a quick jog, either back to my car, or if I have more time a longer jog around the beautiful landscape I've been swimming in.
>
> Beth: Some star jumps once I've managed to dry myself off – then join Hannah for a jog.

Carding Mill Valley

ANNIE BROOKS,
Leicestershire
Blogger at Tales of Annie Bean & owner of For Every Adventure
ITSANNIEBEAN

I remember loving to swim as a child but lost touch with it until 2014 when I entered my first triathlon. I needed to learn how to open-water swim and do front crawl. It is safe to say I've been hooked on open water swimming ever since! It's my meditation.

SWIM PATCH:
THE MIDLANDS

People tend to think the Midlands are mainly built-up areas, but I actually live in a very green area with some beautiful swim spots.

River Soar, Mountsorrel
soups.generated.sleeping

Just off the A6 Granite Way roundabout you'll find a road with a walkway gate on the left-hand side, opposite the entrance to the village; through there you'll have a short walk across the field to one of my favourite wild swim spots. This is a regular spot for the local wild swim group, the Leicestershire Dragonflies (find them on Facebook), where many meet up and swim together.

Anchor Church, Milton
resonates.retire.emperor

Anchor Church, a World Heritage site that sits right next to the River Trent, is the place to find incredible caves. To get to this great swim spot, you'll need to walk from the main road (foiled.wired.

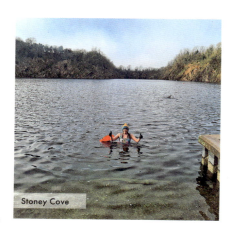
Stoney Cove

Mountsorrel

extremely) over fields, but it is worth the steps. If doing this in winter, it gets extremely muddy so wear appropriate footwear and watch out for the cows!

With the Anchor Church swim area in particular, you need to be careful of the current of the River Trent. Anchor Church has no through water, but just over the bridge the river can be quite strong and sometimes unpredictable. If you're keen to swim on that side, a beautiful location where many wild swimmers regularly go, be sure to swim with others to be super safe. There's an organised swim event on this stretch called the Trent 12k.

Stoney Cove
📍 **shuffle.purely.swordfish**

An incredible, old, enclosed quarry where you swim in spring-fed water with scuba-divers. One thing I absolutely love is how clear the water is and because it is so deep you have no weed issues. There's a 1 kilometre course around the perimeter and a boat on standby for rescues. On site is a café called Nemo's that does great sandwiches and hot drinks for getting that post-swim warmth.

IMOGEN RADFORD,
East Anglia
Outdoor Swimming Society inland access officer
🌐 IMOGENSRIVERSWIMS.CO.UK/BLOG

I like swimming in rivers. I did it as a child and rediscovered it in 2012, from reading Roger Deakin's *Waterlog*. I revisited places where he swam and discovered places where others swim, and started finding new places myself.

SWIM PATCH:
EAST ANGLIA

East Anglia has many lovely swimming rivers in the broad valleys – the Wensum, the Waveney, and more. Most of them are chalk streams and though it isn't always easy to get access to the water, when you can find a spot it is a delight to bask in the slow-moving water, plan a swim journey in a tidal river, or play (with care) in the white water of a mill race. There are numerous beautiful and very swimmable lakes, but few of them allow access to swim.

Ebridge Mill, North Walsham & Dilham Canal
📍 ratio.verifying.inclines

A large basin with fairly shallow water, though there are possibilities to jump in, and also the option to swim about a mile upstream. Lovely walks can be taken by the canal and in the nearby Bacton Wood and there are electric boat trips at certain times.

Don't let the word 'canal' put you off – it is really a clean river, though rather slow-flowing, so can sometimes be slightly murky and occasionally weedy, but usually the canal trust keeps the weeds cleared. The trust (nwdct.org) is restoring it as a canal that welcomes swimmers, anglers, paddleboards, model boating, walkers – and all share the space amicably.

There is space for parking, but availability varies if there is canal restoration work going on – best to check the trust's Facebook in advance – but nearby parking is possible, too. The mill is about two miles from North Walsham, at the far northwest corner of the Broads; it is reached by very small lanes and can be a little hard to find.

The converted mill has a number of flats, but residents are used to seeing

Hellesdon Mill

people using the water, so there are no particular sensitivities, other than the usual respectful behaviour. Local swimmers have joined the trust to support it, and some volunteer to help in conservation work. There is a lovely page dedicated to swimming on their website.

Entry points to the water can vary. At the end of the island is a shallow gravel entry, with a sometimes muddy slope to get down, or you can get in by a low brick wall. Or enter by the sometimes muddy banks on the west side of the pool. There is a platform for paddleboarders, but this can't be used when the model boaters are there.

Hellesdon Mill, Norwich
◉ prep.remark.caves

A popular picnic place with a mill pool, shallow water, then deeper stretches further downstream. If you go up the other side of the island there is another weir pool further upstream where young people have been known to jump in!

Long walks and cycle rides are possible on the Marriott's Way, which runs in a big loop from central Norwich to Aylsham. If not arriving by bicycle, on foot or by river, parking is quite limited in the car park, which has a height barrier, and on Mill Lane (please consider the local residents). Entry from near the car park is very easy into shallow gravelly water.

It is also possible to approach the river from the Marriott's Way across the meadow to the west of the river, following winding paths that take you to the upper pool. It can be very popular and busy in summer – with anglers and canoes and kayaks – so be sensitive to numbers and to local residents and the wildlife. Take the usual care in the white water in the mill pool and weir pool. Water flow can vary.

River Waveney

Outney Meadow
📍 expectant.consonant.fastening

An enormous area of common land in a big loop of the delightful River Waveney, near Bungay. You can walk from the town, or arrive by canoe. There are lots of walks around the common and beyond, on the Angles Way.

There is a car park (manage.equivocal.crops), which can get full on a busy day. Walk across the meadow towards the river and find somewhere to get in. There is a popular place with a rope swing and jump-in spot called the Sandy, which you might find by hearing youthful happy cries, though the sound might also be coming from the Outney Meadow caravan park (outneymeadow.co.uk) – open only to those staying – which also has a rope swing and hires out canoes

This is a well-known place, without many houses nearby, but please be sensitive to wildlife and livestock, and take the usual responsible attitude. The water is deep and clear, though some stretches have weeds in summer. It can be crowded with canoeists and young people jumping in, but there is plenty of room for everyone. Some entry points are a bit tricky – walk along the river until you find somewhere you can get in, and more importantly out again. Refreshments are available in the town, about 20 minutes' walk away.

Geldeston Locks Inn, Beccles
◉ **nodded.spans.wallet**

A lovely deep stretch of the River Waveney, reached at the end of a long track to the isolated pub, recently taken over by the community. It is nearly at the top end of the tidal reach of this river, and boats can moor in the disused lock. People jump from the bridge in summer, and the area can flood in winter. Swimming is in the main part of the river near the footbridge.

There is a car park for the pub, a little way back from the river, and it can be reached by footpath from Beccles either through fields from the south, or along the river. Or arrive by ferry (bigdogferry.co.uk) from Beccles Lido (beccleslido.com) or hire a canoe from there.

Be aware that the tide can make a difference if you are canoeing, also to entry in and more importantly getting out of the water. Exit from the water at this location is not easy, and is particularly difficult at low tide – unless you have good upper body strength. There are ladders in the lock, but you need to be wary of using these when there are boats coming and going. Also, as the water in the lock doesn't move much there can be algal blooms in summer. Look up tide times for Gorleston here – it's four hours behind Gorleston. Don't forget to stop for refreshments at the Locks Inn.

Wainford Silo, Broome
◉ **facelift.coast.solid**

Just east of Bungay, a small meadow near the distinctive tall, white silo building. Swimming is best upstream of the weir, as the weir pool is weedy and the white water fierce. Parking is limited, and you need to be considerate of the houses nearby. There is no easy access by bicycle or on foot, though there are some nice lanes between there and Geldeston and Beccles. Despite its small size, the road can become a busy cut-through.

Water entry is easy, from a canoe portage platform into shallow water, to the left and upstream of the weir. Swim upstream from the weir into deep and occasionally weedy water. Be aware that some jump from structures and from trees. The pool below the weir is not especially dangerous if you keep away from the white water, but it isn't very nice and is often weedy in summer.

Shingle Street

BELLA BRYSON & BEN DAVIES,
Suffolk
Physiotherapist (Bella)
Sports PR manager (Ben)
BENELLASWIMS

We fell in love through our love of water. Bella had been wild swimming for years when we met. On my birthday in March 2018, she persuaded me to go for a dip at Waldringfield. It was a beautiful sunny day and I fell in love with it, so much so that since then we have swum together regularly in the River Deben and the North Sea. In 2020 we did a fundraising challenge for Parkinson's UK, in memory of my grandfather who had the disease, to swim a kilometre every weekend outdoors. We swam whatever the weather and with no wetsuits.

SWIM PATCH:
SUFFOLK

River Deben, Waldringfield
bells.dispensed.superbly

About four miles from where we live and within the Suffolk Coast and Heaths area of outstanding natural beauty, this was where we had our first date. Next to the wonderful Maybush pub, there is a car park. You can walk to the beach from the back of it, down the steps past the beach huts. This is an estuary, though, so pay attention to the tides and note that the current in the main boating channel is fast flowing; stay within the buoys which mark a safe area for swimming by the shore.

Shingle Street
rivals.tequila.casually

At the mouth of the River Ore, a single, remote line of cottages leads down not just to a shingle street but a whole vast beach of shingle. These buildings were originally home to fishermen and river pilots. Two small car parks are located just off the main road and, once parked, you'll need to walk over the stones towards the beach. You'll notice the Martello tower, built to protect England from invasion during the Napoleonic wars. Be careful when swimming here, as on your left (when looking at the sea) the River Deben meets the sea, so it can be really rough. And don't swim out beyond the buoys, as powerful currents can drag you out.

HARRIET CARR & SARAH BANE,
Norwich
Swimming instructors
SWIMSPOTSNORFOLK

We have both been in the world of swimming since a very young age, from training with a club, competing, working as lifeguards and teaching people how to swim. Sarah's expertise is with babies and young children. Harriet has predominantly taught secondary school children and also specialises in coaching adults.

SWIM PATCH:
NORWICH

From the city of Norwich, a trip to the beach is within an hour's drive in any direction. We are spoilt for choice with our coastline, with every beach location offering a different experience, from the Jurassic cliffs at Overstrand beach, to the offshore rock bars at Sea Palling, and the pristine, hidden gem that is Long Beach.

> ## ESSENTIAL KIT
> A swim buddy!
> I am a competent swimmer, but never swim without a buddy, despite being a qualified lifeguard and swim instructor.

Anderson's Meadow
forest.sizes.king

In the heart of the city, Anderson's Meadow is a green patch of escapism, situated between the busy Drayton Road and Mile Cross Road. The entry point, opposite the Eagle canoe club, allows you to use a slipway to acclimatise to the water, before pushing off the wooden ledge into the deep waters of the River Wensum. Kayakers, canoeists, picnicking families and teenage dippers tend to stay in the Anderson's Meadow vicinity. For the more avid swimmer, travelling east towards the city will take you on a beautiful waterway journey to Wensum Park, where it is possible to exit the water with ease. The urban ducks and geese do seem a little perplexed seeing you in their stretch of water. The residents in the row of townhouses along Wensum View Gardens might also seem a little stunned, but they tend to wave from their windows or even pop onto their balconies for a morning chat. As this section of the River Wensum doesn't accommodate boats, reeds and waterweeds do exist. You are completely immersed in nature at this swim spot, despite being in the centre of Norwich.

Park your car or bike at the local Lidl or Aldi supermarkets on Drayton Road, then walk through to Marriott's Way. I always buy myself a pastry or a sweet treat as a post swim snack.

Sea Palling
📍 **freshest.dude.folds**

This swimming spot, 19.5 miles northeast of Norwich, is well worth the day trip. As soon as you climb the dunes away from the low-lying land, the hustle and bustle of the fine city is replaced with unspoilt natural beauty and fresh sea air. A flood-prevention scheme saw offshore rock bars built, where sand links the bars to the shore at low tide. It is at low tide when it is possible to swim adjacent to the shoreline, between the reefs.

Visitors to Sea Palling often park in Clink Lane, as it's handy for the shops on Beach Road. For those seeking total escapism, travel further along the Marrams and park for free behind the dunes approximately a mile away. Several discreet sandy footpaths lead to the beach, a little further along from the main stretch of beach. The downside is that this area of the beach is not lifeguard patrolled. The upside is a much quieter section of coastline.

Swim laps between two rock bars or use the sand links to run or walk back to the starting position and repeat. Don't be alarmed if you stop for a rest halfway through your swim and see a head pop up in your direction. It is not uncommon to swim alongside seals, which venture inside the rock bars. They are simply inquisitive and will not trouble you if you keep on swimming. Do take in the moment if you do encounter a seal, as it is a truly magical experience.

Sea Palling

Cleve Prior

PENNY WILKIN & EMMA O'BRIEN,
Warwickshire
Authors of Dips and Chips
DIPSANDCHIPSTHEBOOK

Emma is an illustrator and artist and combines her love of drawing with her passion for swimming. Penny is a triathlete, so she enjoys cycling and running outdoors as well as swimming.

During the Covid-19 pandemic, when pools were closed, we needed to find a wider variety of places to swim outdoors – for our sanity and physical well-being. Once we were allowed to travel again after restrictions were relaxed, we rediscovered the power of a weekly watery tonic in the countryside. After finding some amazing places to swim on our doorstep that we didn't know existed, we decided to write our own guidebook to share the benefits of wild swimming. And *Dips and Chips* was born.

SWIM PATCH:
WARWICKSHIRE & THE RIVER AVON

Warwickshire is surrounded by large conurbations such as Birmingham and Coventry. It's quite far from the sea and isn't known for having a lot of lakes or places to swim. This is what makes the places we swim at even more special, because it's a rarity and almost a surprise to find somewhere.

The Avon is generally a very friendly river for swimmers, as it's relatively small compared to, say, the Wye or the Severn.

> ### WARM UP TIP
> Wear a thick, giant bobble hat. The bigger the better! Don't bother with underwear – too much faff.

This means it's swimmable most of the year round, even for head-up breaststroke, unless its flooded owing to heavy rainfall – but you should always check the flow before getting in.

River Avon, Marlcliff
◉ supplied.bead.magpie

Marlcliff is a tiny Warwickshire hamlet with stunning thatched cottages on the River Avon. Take a little lane on the bend off the B4085 called The Bank. This takes you into the hamlet but it's a dead-end. Look out for beautifully kept lawns, a stunning little thatched cottage, a weeping willow on the left and a bench on the right. In between, on the left-hand side, is a small gravel track. If you miss it, you'll end up at a dead-end in the heart of the hamlet.

The gravel track takes you down to an opening by the river with plenty of parking space. On a summer's day, it can be busy; there's also a field behind the hedge that people use. The river has super easy access with a couple of fishing platforms to lower yourself from, or you can wade in from the bank to the side of the platforms. Once in the river there are reeds on either side so it feels quiet and secluded. See if you can spot the church tower in the distance on the opposite side. A public footpath runs all the way to Bidford on Avon, so it can be busy but I enjoy seeing people out in the countryside. It also makes a great place to take non-swimming friends who might like to walk alongside while you swim.

River Avon, Cleve Prior
◉ courtyard.coasters.faced

Once parked on Mill Lane, Evesham (tops.salary.myths), go through the gap on the left-hand side of the gate into a cute little field with picnic benches. Walk down the riverbank and you'll discover the perfect hidden swim spot. There's a delightful bench on some wooden decking, which looks like it's been designed exactly for swimming, but is more likely to be a fishing platform.

Getting into the river off the platform could be a bit tricky because of its height above the water and sharp-looking edges, but this will depend on how tall you are and the river levels. It might be easier to look to the side of the platform and get in using the riverbank and the edge of the platform as support. As you look at the river, upstream is to the right. You'll swim towards a weeping willow and some ruined farm buildings on the opposite bank, which give that taken-back-in-time feeling. Downstream is to the left and on the opposite bank you can see Abbots Salford Holiday Park.

The river is beautiful and deep with plenty of room to swim properly, including getting some distance in for a fitness training swim if you wanted to. The flow is quite strong. Be sure to check it before you go anywhere.

Welford-on-Avon
📍 bibs.headers.delight

Welford-on-Avon is a stunning village of 17th-century timber thatched cottages; it also has a 14th-century church. It's worth having a little walk around this beautiful village to see the church and the associated vicarage.

It's a few minutes' walk from the village to the river. If driving, park at Church Street (clinked.absorbing.dairy). Walk to the end of Boat Lane and turn right to go upstream and walk along the footpath, past the weir until you find a suitable place to get in upstream of the black barrels that mark the weir. You'll see a beautiful wide stretch of river ideal for swimming. There are lots of fishing spots, gaps in the grass with neat little benches, which, on first inspection, look like the perfect places to get in. However, the banks are very steep and the river is immediately deep. It's always easy to get in, but check the depth and make sure you can get out. There's a footpath along the riverside, so while it's a popular spot for dog walkers and joggers it's still beautifully quiet and tranquil.

POST SWIM SNACK

Emma's vegan Biscoff Cake (see page 83).

CLARE ALLEN,
Cambridgeshire
Vet
📷 CLAREVET

A few years ago, I had a yearning to get back in the water again. I can't say exactly why that was, but after I started swimming I continued doing it and it felt right. I had been having a lot of pain related to land exercise, running in particular, which was later diagnosed as psoriatic arthritis, an immune disease. Whenever I went for a run or a walk, I would be in pain afterwards and often very fatigued. What I discovered about cold water was, firstly, I was pain-free when I got in and, secondly, I felt better for days after. It was almost like a body-sense that this was what I was supposed to do.

SWIM PATCH:
CAMBRIDGESHIRE

Grantchester Meadows
📍 **sparks.jacket.scuba**

Swimming in this stretch of the Cam, in the village of Grantchester, south of Cambridge, feels like swimming through history. Here, Cambridge students and locals, town and gown, have taken a dip for over a century – war poet Rupert Brooke swam there, as did Lord Byron, and Byron's Pool is by a weir in the river. That history is one of the reasons why, when King's College, who own the land on either side of the river, announced a ban on swimming there, the outdoor swimming community here were quick to protest and the ban was lifted.

The biggest problem with Grantchester Meadows in terms of access is that its banks are very eroded, very steep in places, or muddy in others where the cows, a feature of the meadows, get in and out. These issues were one reason that King's College proposed the ban. It's also why people have created their own access points. The best place to enter is at Dead Man's Corner, where a stepladder is jammed into the silt and mud. From this lovely spot, you can swim down past the membership-only Newnham Riverbank Club (joinable strictly by introduction!) – whose secret garden and fenced-off grounds sit on its banks – all the way to Sheep's Green and Lammas Land. There is also a canoe club at Sheep's Green where you can get in and out.

One of the joys of Grantchester Meadows is how it's right in the heart of the city – a really lovely bit of nature, that has long been accessible to everybody, from which you can have a river's eye view.

There are two public rights of way along Grantchester Meadow: the cycle path that cuts straight across and the meandering footpath that goes along the riverbank. Parking is available at Lammas Land or on-street; it's also possible to take a bus into the centre of Cambridge and walk from there.

odd narrowboat chugging up and down.

I've swum there through all four seasons and that's been really meaningful – you feel like you get to know the swans and the ducks. The current gets quite strong after heavy rain, because not only does the river fill up but the sluice gates are opened further up, so avoid swimming then. We always swim upstream and then swoosh back down.

Enter at the slipway, which is public access – a council sign makes this clear – and runs between parts of the pub garden. Only use the pub car park if you intend on being a good patron – otherwise park in the village and simply walk down.

The Cam, Upware
📍 **dignity.stockpile.feelers**

The fact that access to this beautiful, wild stretch of the Cam is via a slipway next to a pub called the Five Miles From Anywhere says a great deal. The village of Upware is little more than two streets, a marina and a pub, surrounded by vast stretches of fens. Though the pub, whose large beer garden – the perfect spot for a post-swim drink – can get busy in summer, once you immerse yourself in the river and swim round the bend you soon find you're out in the middle of nature. Often I have it to myself, just me and the ducks and the geese and a solitary heron, perhaps the

Upware

REBECCA WARD,
Cotswolds
Swim coach & river conservation volunteer
📷 WARDENOFLOVE

About six years ago, some mums at my sons' school were training for a triathlon, and said, 'Come along; we have tea and cake afterwards.' I thought I was going for the tea and cake, but when I got there I had to borrow a wetsuit. I was terrified of swimming in the sea and lakes. But something about it – it was a beautiful, sunny September day – meant that at some point I stopped panicking. I remember thinking, this is really cool, I'll do it again . . . and then it became an obsession. I realised I was slightly calmer and wasn't having so many bouts of depression.

SWIM PATCH:
COTSWOLDS

This beautiful area is home to the Cotswold waterparks, an expanse of a hundred lakes, only a few of which are used for recreation and swimming, including the lake I normally swim in, Lake 32. But there are also plenty of opportunities for river swims, too, on the Thames, which flows from its source in the Cotswold Hills.

Neigh Bridge Country Park
📍 easily.homelands.bronzes

On the Young Thames, only about three miles from its source, there is a delightful, narrow, crystal-clear stretch which is what's called a winterbourne – it dries up in about May, and is only a swimming spot in winter and spring. I started swimming there about two weeks after lockdown began in 2020. The stretch is very clean and clear. There is a slight bend in the river so you've got a maximum amount of space to swim up against the flow and swoosh back again. A deep pool has also been carved here on the bend, so you can jump and dive and bomb in (but make sure you get in and check for hazards first). There's a little car park (hiker.only.deeds) just a short walk away, so it's good for pitching up with the kids and carrying all your kit over. We found it to hit the sweet spot between feeling like you're in this idyllic spot in the wild – there's snowdrops growing and beautiful trees – but being quite close to a car park and not too far off the beaten track. One of the beauties of this winter location is that it will always be relatively quiet – because the number of people swimming in the winter months is always going to be fewer.

Thames Path, Kemble
◉ soft.clauses.marathons

Park at the little Thames Path car park (fewer.stray.counts) just off the main road before you get into the village of Kemble. One of the great things about this spot is it's on the Thames Path and publicly accessible. I wanted to find places that I was comfortable advertising to other members of the Lake community and I don't like to recommend places where you have to trespass. From this parking spot you follow the Thames footpath along the edge of a field eastwards until you find a stretch of the Young Thames on a bend with trees surrounding. It's really pretty. We've done quite a lot of our moonlit swims there because it's not too close to civilisation and we can skinny dip. We like to swing a hammock up between the trees, and there are even some tree roots that you can walk down into the water as if they were a set of steps.

Cheesewharf, Lechlade
◉ panthers.speeded.quieter

Just outside Lechlade, on a bend in the Thames, used to be a wharf where West Country cheese would be loaded up on barges bound for London – and we can now swim at Cheesewharf. The area is the National Trust's Buscot and Coleshill estate, and it's a great place to watch the sunrise, as the sun comes up over the poplar trees opposite the little National Trust car park (whistle.officer.craftsman).

Because it's a more mature part of the Thames the flow is slightly faster, so caution is advised after rainfall. But it's not so fast that you can't swim against the flow and make a bit of headway. Lechlade itself is a beautiful place – known as the gateway to the Cotswolds – with nice coffee shops, including the gorgeous Lynwood & Co., with its sourdough and artisan cakes.

There are a few spots along that stretch of river where you can pop along and swim or paddleboard, so people do point-to-point swims there. You can get in with your dry bag and a towel and potentially leave one car at one point and one at another.

Neigh Bridge Country Park

SAFETY TIP

I always say it's not knowing when to swim, it's being strong and brave enough on a day that it doesn't feel right to say, I'm not going to. Because it's really hard if you've packed all your kit up, you've got someone to look after the kids . . . You have to have that wherewithal to say something isn't right and not do it.

Clifton Hampden Bridge

Longbridges

KATIA VASTIAU,
Marsh Baldon, Oxford
Social media & marketing professional
BELGOKATIA

I learned to swim late. I was ten years old, but took to it immediately and spent a decade as a club and a Belgian national team swimmer, making the early Barcelona pre-selection in breaststroke before damaging my knee at the age of 17. After that I spent twenty years out of the water doing important life things like moving to another country, university, parties, sports, jobs and having a family. Once my kids were older and craving time in the house without me, I felt it was the perfect time to return to swimming. I was 38 and 'fell' into open water almost straight away. I am happiest under, on or in the water and have made some amazing friends there too!

SWIM PATCH:
OXFORDSHIRE

For a landlocked area, Oxfordshire is actually a little heaven for outdoor swimmers. We might not have the sea, but the county cradles the Thames Valley, and we have quite a few lakes dotted around. Wildlife is plentiful, with water birds and small bank mammals a common occurrence, and it's always lovely to see red kites gliding overhead too.

Oxford has a history of rowing, of course, but the river used to be a big swimming social place, with bathing spots dotted around and some of those still have structures standing. The Thames is lovely to swim in throughout the year, but its swimability is weather-dependent, and the Upper Thames is prone to flooding, often in the winter months, both over and beyond the flood plain. This, plus the resulting high water levels and fast flow, as well as the potential waterworks overflow after heavy rain, can restrict swimming at times.

Clifton Hampden Bridge
supporter.scrambles.bubble

A picture-perfect spot that offers very easy access by road and ample parking options that won't disturb residents, as well as a pretty red-brick bridge to swim

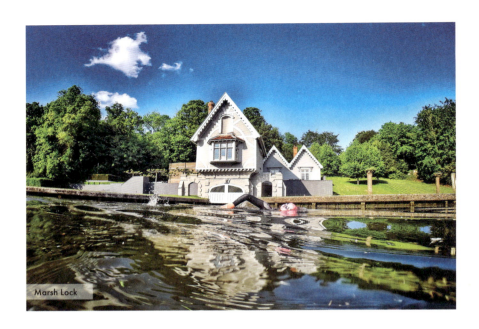
Marsh Lock

through. There's a shop that welcomes swimmers, sells essentials including a good selection of cakes and basic hot drinks, plus fresh local fruit in season too.

Park in the layby just past the post office or, if it's busy, carry on over the bridge to the other side of the river and use the car park across from the Barley Mow pub, which is a public one. You can either access the water on the side of the layby, by walking until you reach two clear entry points where the grass gets a bit worn, or take the footpath starting just after the bridge on the opposite bank (be careful of the pair of swans who nest around there every year).

Swim about 400 metres upstream under the bridge and towards the lock, then hang a left and take the cut that bypasses the lock and finishes as a very quiet dead-end about 1.5 kilometres further, passing a big house with boat house and even a pub accessible from the water. From there, you can just turn back and take in the scenery in reverse.

When the water reaches a decent temperature, I like to pack my running or walking clothes and towel in my tow float and head downstream. It is a beautiful 5 kilometres (or so) to Day's Lock in Little Wittenham. Geese, swans, ducks, herons, kingfishers and cows are the usual suspects on this stretch and a couple of old pillboxes from the Second World War too.

Marsh Lock, Henley-on-Thames
◈ greyhound.warbler.waters

From the Marsh Lock car park, walk the few minutes to the lock, then over the beautiful long wooden bridge towards the meadow. A few hundred yards upstream you will find several little shallow entry beaches, allowing you to get into the river safely.

Here you need to swim upstream and away from the lock towards Shiplake. After the first corner you will come to two islands that make for good swimming destinations. You can swim up to and around them, then reach a further island upstream before you arrive at Shiplake, with houses and boats moored on the banks. Swimming on the left is best, so you can see boats approaching and tuck into the side accordingly.

Here, you're not far from the centre of Henley, where there are plenty of little cafés. A short walk, 500 metres from the first access point, usually earns you peace and quiet. You won't disturb any residents either.

Longbridges, Oxford
◈ strut.adults.join

Access is by foot or cycle along the Thames Path from Donnington Bridge, or from Weirds Lane and the nearest free public car park is off Meadow Lane.

Longbridges, now part of a nature reserve, is very near the centre of town yet it's slightly tucked away on the backwaters of the River Thames, away from the main stretch which gets really busy with rowers and punters. It also used to be the largest open-air bathing place in Oxford (closed in 1980), and if you look carefully you can still see the concrete remains of the edges of the pool and the base of the changing facilities and one of the pool ladders.

Further away from the old bathing site, you find yourself in more overgrown and greener surroundings and you can easily find a nice spot to get in and out. Where it gets deeper, after a good check, you can take a few dives in from fallen trees or swim towards the little weir. As always, with weirs, keep safe. This one is small and gives the feel of an endless pool from a distance but don't swim too close when the flow is up.

JONATHAN COWIE,
Kendal
Editor, Outdoor Swimmer
🅸 JONNYHCOWIE

Twelve years ago I did the mile swim at the Great North Swim. I was hooked straight away – and I am now the editor of *Outdoor Swimmer* magazine! I love all kinds of outdoor swimming, from ice dipping to marathon swims. Having lived in London for nearly 25 years, I have a soft spot for an urban wild swim, but I now live close to Windermere, where my outdoor swimming journey began.

SWIM PATCH:
LONDON

Think of wild swimming and London probably isn't the first location that pops into your head. But our capital city is brimming with opportunities to swim outdoors, from lidos to ponds to the River Thames. There is something special about urban wild swimming – the thrill of the unexpected, the juxtaposition of nature and the built environment. It somehow feels more daring to be taking to the waters when all around you the city bustles about its everyday business.

Love Open Water, London Royal Docks
📍 **aspect.zebra.lend**

Surrounded by skyscrapers and high-rise flats, London Royal Docks is the most urban of urban swimming spots. Overhead the Emirates cable car whisks tourists from the docks to the Greenwich Peninsula, while planes take off from City Airport. To swim here is a real London experience. It is open all year round and in the winter you can swim in the dark with an illuminated tow float. Imagine floating in the cold water, watching the lights of Canary Wharf and the City twinkle in the

POST SWIM WARM UP

Dancing! Throwing some shapes is the best way to warm up.

night sky. In summer there is a kilometre loop so you can get some real distance in.

Post-swim drinks at the Oiler Bar are a Docks tradition or head to the Crystal Café for excellent and reasonably priced food. Book your swim on the Actio app (NOWCA wristband required).

Bushes Outside Simon's House, Teddington Lock
◉ tigers.casual.flies

In lockdown, with pools, lidos and fitness venues closed, Londoners had few swimming options. But one spot in southwest London, near Teddington Lock, became a mecca for the city's landlocked swimmers. And even with lockdown over, it remains a popular spot for urban swimmers who like their dipping on the wild side.

Easily reached by bike, the entry point into the river is coincidentally opposite *Outdoor Swimmer* founder Simon Griffith's house (hence its name, often abbreviated to BOSH). Get changed by two benches overlooking the river and swim either across or upstream against the current. Don't swim downstream as there is a weir. Alternatively, walk upstream to a small concrete jetty by the YWCA Hawker Centre and swoosh back down (especially fun when the river is in full flow!).

Afterwards, walk downstream and cross the footbridge for coffee and cake at the Flying Cloud Café or a drink and something more substantial at the Anglers pub.

Beckenham Place Park Lake
◉ risky.lend.pinks

The suburban reaches of southeast London aren't synonymous with wild swimming, but a small lake in Beckenham Place Park is a bucolic idyll. This new, purpose-built swimming venue (it opened in summer 2019) is surrounded by parkland and – if you ignore the ugly metal fence – you could be in the depths of the countryside rather than in the borough of Lewisham. Reeds and bullrushes surround the lake and you will share your swim with ducks as well as a friendly community of swimmers.

Grab a coffee and cake after your swim at the Homestead Café or head further up the hill in the park to Beckenham Place Mansion, which has a bar and café, as well as playing host to events such as food and vintage markets, concerts and pop-up cinemas. If you like running, the Beckenham Place Park Parkrun is signposted, so you can easily follow the 5 kilometres route.

Book your swim at ptpcoaching.co.uk.

Glovers Island

Beckenham Place Park Lake

Petersham Meadows

EMMA RICHARDS,
Hampton
Freelance copywriter
📷 SWIMWRITEM

My swim odyssey began as a result of a painful breakdown a couple of years ago. I did my very first open water swim at Shepperton Lake and then fell in with a group of mermaids called Surrey Outdoor Swimmers who took me under their wing. One lady, Ju, was incredible. She introduced me to the medicinal powers of 'Dr Thames' and talked me through the dark times. This selfless bunch have brought light, love and laughter back into my life. I'm now a Mental Health Swims co-host with swim buddy @mhshampton and I am a qualified open water swim coach with Straight Line Swimming.

SWIM PATCH:
RIVER THAMES

Hampton
📍 **grapes.cats.then**

During lockdown, Hampton was my 'go-to' place. It's one of the most scenic stretches of the Thames, combining natural beauty and literary heritage. This river idyll is straight out of Kenneth Grahame's *The Wind in the Willows*. You can enter at the steps by the acid-green willow, swim downstream past Garrick's Temple to Shakespeare and marvel at the iconic Astoria houseboat (built in 1911) where Laurel and Hardy stayed. You've got everything you could possibly need for the perfect river swim – colourful houseboats, lush reeds to a vast array of wildlife from herons and crested grebes, Egyptian geese and local celebrity 'Sid the Swan' (named after Sid Vicious for a reason).

Sunbury-on-Thames
📍 **arts.unions.goal**

Park next to Indian Zest restaurant and enter the river under the great plane tree at Sunbury Meadow, just over the pedestrian footbridge, on Rivermead Island, adjacent to Molesey lock. This is a great location for beginners because there's a gently shelving beach which provides a good entry and exit point and there's even a couple of benches to give you changing space. It's a seasonal swim with options. In winter, walk up the high street and swoosh back from the Flowerpot pub, then treat yourself with a curry at Indian Zest. In summer, arrive early and bring a picnic and a rug. Or, better still, make a date with dawn and try a magical sunrise swim. Apart from a few fisherfolk you will have the river to yourselves and you may even catch a glimpse of the resident kingfisher. A yew tree within the parish churchyard of St Mary was even mentioned in Dickens's *Oliver Twist* (its nave dates back to 1752), so you're in good company.

Thames Ditton
📍 **party.eggs.likes**

Enter in by the Albany pub (Aragon Avenue) near Thames Ditton Rowing Club and change by the bench opposite the resplendent riverside golden gates of Hampton Court Palace (built in 1515). There's a sandy, shelving beach which allows you to wade gently in – and offers good entry and exit points. In summer, Surrey Outdoor Swimmers organise Friday night swims up to Hampton Court Bridge, where you can swim in petal-velvet water under a midnight sky lit with tangerine tow floats. It's about a mile (there and back) and you will get an intimate view of the Palace. If you coincide a swim with the Palace Festival, music concerts and fireworks will be thrown in for free. A special, historic swim.

Petersham Meadows, Richmond
📍 **turned.frames.yard**

Park at Ham House riverside car park and you are five minutes' stroll from this tidal stretch of the Thames. Get in opposite the White Swan pub. Here, the wide neck of the river winds through lush vegetation and tall trees line the banks like kings. If you listen to the sound of the parakeets it feels almost Amazonian. Passing the Palladian villa of Marble Hill House, you'll emerge further downstream at Petersham Meadows. Gaze up towards Richmond Hill and marvel at where Turner painted his famous view of the Thames. You can either exit at the meadows and walk back or swim all the way to Richmond Bridge. We did this swim at midsummer and camped out late, feasting on chilli and chocolate brownies under the gaze of the moon.

> **ESSENTIAL KIT**
>
> My pink Toncho, lightweight fast-drying changing robe – perfect for packing in your tow float and made of recycled plastic.

DAWN STEELE,
Whitstable
Actor

I live by the coast and had long swum in the sea in the summer but had always wanted to swim all year round. I just didn't have the courage. Then one day, a friend at my daughter's school mentioned they had started and did I want to join them? That was it. I loved it from that first exhilarating moment. I started at the sea's coldest point with no wetsuit (later I invested in the gloves, boots and dryrobe obviously). I really embraced the cold. Come the summer months when the sea is warm(ish), it's more about a longer swim for the exercise, but I feel I get more out of the short dips in the windy wild winter sea!

SWIM PATCH:
WHITSTABLE

Whitstable is a bay that lies to the east of the outlet of the Swale into the Thames Estuary. We are at the behest of the tides. I love to swim in the morning and evening; sunrise and sunset are my favourite times in Whitstable. The sunsets are amazing, but if I swim in the morning it sets me up for the day. It's generally sunny and warm, but the sea can be rough, though not often – and I love that too. It doesn't get too busy, especially when it's snowing in January! We sometimes get some jellyfish and I'm stung all the time somehow. Even so, I never want to leave this town! We are really lucky to live here.

Tankerton Beach
📍 edges.glee.device

This is across the road from my house so it's just a walk into the sea. Looking out to the beach huts on one side and the empty horizon on the other, you might see the famous Whitstable sea forts which were built to provide anti-aircraft fire in the war in 1942 – this is where the men slept and kept watch – or even a few seals.

There are toilets here and, further along, there's a lifeguard hut and some outdoor taps and showers (not many, though!). Head to JoJo's for lunch after or go get a coffee in town, or a takeaway from Grain & Hearth in Whitstable.

Walpole Tidal Pool, Margate
📍 belly.feast.monks

Great for a change from the open sea. A tidal pool feels so different, as you have not got the pull of the sea but you are still in that glorious salty water! It also works if you can't fit in a swim around high tide. Margate is full of amazing places to eat and drink (Forts coffee shop is the best for coffee and cake) and it's worth a trip to the Turner Gallery (not in your dryrobe obviously!). No toilets here, though.

POST SWIM DRINK

Gimber and hot water (expensive!) – otherwise a hot herbal tea in a flask in an enamel mug, as it heats up your hands.

Tankerton Beach

SUS DAVY,
Bath
Café owner
ROUGHMEASURES

I was born and raised in Bath. Growing up near the Avon, we often swam along the river. The water has always, and still does, given me a sense of calm and stillness that I crave. Last year, I became a founding member of the Bath Open Water Beauts – a community for those who love a cold water dip or swim.

SWIM PATCH:
BATH

The River Avon runs through Bath and there are multiple locations with decent access to get into the water. I love the fact that I can stop somewhere on my commute to or from work and have a swim. I love the plethora of nature and wildlife that runs along the Avon. Having water so readily accessible nearby is one of the reasons I have stayed living in Bath.

Warleigh Weir
diary.bother.rope

Warleigh is a classic wild swimming spot. It has grown in popularity over the years, and really is a special place. A large weir cuts through the river and it is rather a showstopper. We often see herons and kingfishers there. The landowner for Warleigh is actively trying to keep it a pristine nature area, too. Warleigh is not accessible by car and there is no parking, so please don't drive there. Warleigh Weir gets really busy on hot days, so aim to go early in the morning to avoid the crowds. There are no facilities at Warleigh, but the Angelfish Café is a 15-minute walk away.

Farleigh & District Swimming Club
cattle.force.slot

Founded in 1933, the Farleigh & District Swimming Club is believed to be the oldest river swimming club in the country. It's open from May to September and provides changing screens, toilets and a sunbathing field, as well as access to a 70-metre stretch of the River Frome in which you can take a dip. Membership is required, but you can pay when you arrive.

Farleigh

River Avon, Batheaston
📍 **human.woke.notes**

While not the most idyllic of spots, Batheaston has great access for those of us who want to swim in the River Avon. A free car park sits next to the river, making it great for families or those who can't walk far. Stop off afterwards for great fish and chips at Robbie's Plaice.

> **WARM UP TIP**
>
> Dress your top half first and get out of your wet costume as soon as you can.

JOE MINIHANE,
Brighton
Author & journalist
🖂 JOEMINIHANE

My wife and I started swimming at Hampstead about ten years ago and I fell in love with the feeling of calm and sense of wider connection I got after every dip. Then I read Roger Deakin's *Waterlog*. I adore his prose and his approach: singular, anti-authoritarian, fun. So I decided to retrace his journey. This was as much about dealing with my anxiety as it was about following Deakin. I can't imagine life without swimming. It's how I manage my mental wellbeing, how I recharge and how I feel part of something wider and more cosmic. It's a spiritual thing.

SWIM PATCH:
BRIGHTON

I'm lucky enough to live on the seafront in Kemptown. The beach can get wild in winter and busy in summer, but I love how a bike ride in either direction affords you different options. The undercliff towards Saltdean is a dream, with chalk reef beaches and sheltered spots for dips away from the crowds. The cliffs are home to kittiwakes and rock pipits; you might even see a seal. The quality of the light is exceptional, all milky whites and blues.

Cuckmere Haven
📍 smaller.smothered.quack

The oxbow lakes of the meanders of Cuckmere River are a highlight of the area, their brackish water warmer than the sea. It's a popular spot, but the lush hills stretching up to the white chalk Seven Sisters cliffs make it a spectacular place for a languid dip. Park at the Seven Sisters car park in Exceat and access the water close to the main gate. Keep an eye out for submerged objects, SUPs and kayakers.

POST SWIM SNACK

Black coffee and a hot cross bun.

Cuckmere Haven

The water is shallow on the inside bends, so those are the best places to get in.

Ovingdean Beach
📍 **steepest.waggled.musician**

This is on the undercliff path between Brighton Marina and Rottingdean. It's a pebble beach and great for rock pooling at low tide. The little café on the path is perfect for post swim sustenance. Ovingdean's café does great cakes, tea in proper mugs and has a selection of papers for reading on the outdoor seating. There's also a loo.

Essential kit
Neoprene shoes. When you live by a pebble beach, keeping your feet covered becomes second nature.

LORRAINE CANDY,
London
Podcaster & author
LORRAINECANDY

I only learned to swim properly in my late forties, despite growing up in Cornwall by the sea. To say it changed my life is an understatement. For me, open water or wild swimming is about the meditative joy of being in cool or cold water surrounded by nature. I found it extremely helpful for my perimenopause symptoms, and it allowed me to slow down during a relentlessly hectic schedule. 'Take it to the lake' is a phrase my family use all the time when they notice I am not quite myself. And off I go.

SWIM PATCH:
SURREY

Shepperton Lake
push.hulk.actor

I swim here every weekend for as long as it is open throughout the year, which varies. It's roughly a 400 or 800 metre circuit and the small sandy entrance to the lake is banked by beautiful yellow irises in early summer. I feel safe and supported by the wonderfully chirpy team there and also enjoy regular lessons with swim coach Salim Ahmed (page 29), whose gentle persuasion has sped me up on my journey to a more technically correct front crawl. I love the camaraderie of the lake swimmers at Shepperton; they can be triathletes training for an event or slow and steady nature lovers like me, but the friendliness spurs you on especially during the colder months. The 'Wackaexpresso' coffee van, a recent addition to facilities, is a godsend, though we often bring a flask of something hot to warm us up after the swim.

Shepperton is a 45-minute drive on a good day, which goes some way to prove how amazing the experience is, as I live the other side of London but never fail to get there early on a weekend morning to be greeted by the world's friendliest swim venue staff. The relaxed atmosphere and cleanliness of the water is a bonus and catching glimpses of the swan families that live on the lake makes for special memories. I love seeing the plants in the

Shepperton Lake

water below me swaying as I swim.

I have met swimmers from every background at Shepperton and it holds a special place in my heart. Perhaps the day I was a little too cold to get my ancient wetsuit off is a favourite moment – there's nothing like a stranger happily wrestling you out of your neoprene to restore your faith in human kindness.

Essential kit

Often a double hat situation (I like one that goes over the ears in winter), goggles, surf ear plugs (I get a little seasick swimming front crawl without them for some reason), and a dryrobe to change into. Loose, baggy trousers that are easy to slip on if you're not quite dry!

SIMON HARMER,
Hampshire
Speaker & former combat medic
🌐 SIMONHARMER.COM

Everybody has a back story of why planting their face in cold water seems like a good thing. I served just over seventeen years in the British Army as a medic. In my thirteenth year I received life-changing injuries while on foot patrol. I lost both my legs. Open water swimming became an important part of my recovery.

Before I got injured, I was a keen triathlete. Then, afterwards, I was rehabilitating at Henley Court, where all the injured service personnel who came back from Iraq and Afghanistan went to recover. One of the evening activities was to go down to Heron Lake to swim. There would be loads of blokes with no limbs, bits missing, going down there, and I just fell in love with the place.

Swimming made me feel like a normal person again. I could stand up in the water and be straight. In the water, people couldn't see that I didn't have any legs. There was also the social aspect, meeting new people, which really helped. What a lot of people don't realise is that it's a social, community-led activity. Sitting on the floor, getting changed, you could meet literally anyone. They could be famous or simply an everyday person. It's a level playing field.

Open water swimming has made me more resilient. In my situation I have to think about how I'm going to do something and plan how I'm going to achieve it, particularly if I'll have to get out somewhere else. How am I going to marry my kit and my legs and my wheelchair to where I'll get out of the water? I haven't let the fact I've got physical restrictions stop me.

SWIM PATCH: HAMPSHIRE & THE SOUTH

I live in Winchester, which was once the ancient capital of England, and where the M3 goes over the River Itchen, that's where I've been swimming. During lockdown it has been the safest and only location where I've felt comfortable going in. The water's fine. It's just that we're under a motorway bridge.

Heron Lake
◉ **tunes.closes.clash**

It was rehabilitating at Heron Lake that laid the foundation for me to be an open water swimmer. It's just off junction 13 of the M25 and, when you're in the water there, you can see the motorway. When it's really gridlocked and you're in the middle of the lake looking back at the traffic, you feel quite proud of yourself to be there enjoying yourself in the water. Swimming there changed my life and I still swim there now. If I'm ever coming back from somewhere I'll always try and stop there and go for a swim. It holds so much positive stuff from my recovery.

The lake has two courses, one 500 metres and the other 1,000 metres. It's open four days a week and has a NOWCA lake management system, which electronically monitors swimmers coming in

Andark Lake

and out. There are observation and rescue kayaks on the water, too. It's accessible for disabled swimmers and offers a café, wetsuit hire, changing rooms and shop. You can book online at swimheron.co.uk.

Andark Lake
◉ **sunbeam.kitchens.politics**

This is the place where I started my cold water swimming journey. It's actually a dive centre on the south coast, not far from Southampton, and the River Hamble runs past it. In 2019, I wanted a different challenge, so I thought, 'Why don't I try cold water and see, firstly, how my legs can take it (because I've got quite high up amputation on my left leg above the knee and my right leg is quite high amputation below the knee) and, secondly, how my body generally would cope with it?' It was interesting how my body acclimatised. A lot of people say to me now, when I tell them I do skins in cold water, 'I couldn't do that?' I always think, 'Well, I can do it. So, if you wanted to, you could.'

Andark is 60 x 30 metres, and it's actually a dive training area. It's great for new swimmers, because it's a bit smaller, a bit more enclosed. It feels safer. Also, where you enter, it's got ledges for the divers to sit with their tanks, making it easier to get in and out. You've got nothing touching your legs. It's not silty. Of course, if you want to properly swim it's not ideal. And you have to do this sort of weird rectangle swim. If you wanted to do a swim of a kilometre or two, then it's not the place to go.

The lake has changing facilities, lockers, a café. The water is tested regularly and the lake is filled up by its own borehole. Pre-booking is advised at andarklake.co.uk.

Heron Lake

ESSENTIAL KIT

I bought one of the surfer change bags – they're becoming a bit more fashionable now. I use one of those and sit in it – that's been really handy for me. A lot of people get problems with their ears. Recently, on a swim at Test Valley, I asked someone, what do you use? He said BluTac. I use BioWax; it just means I can stay in the water for a lot longer.

ROWAN CLARKE,
Clevedon
Outdoor swimming coach
📷 _FINSANDGOGGLES_

Swimming outdoors has always been a part of my life. My parents and grandmothers loved sea swimming, and there are photos of me as a baby splashing in the breakers. According to my diary when I was four, dipping in the sea was the highlight of my summer holiday in Scotland.

It was thirty years later that I started swimming outdoors in a more meaningful way. By this time, I had three children, and I craved a way to reclaim myself from the demands of pregnancy, childbirth and motherhood. So I entered my first open water swim and got training for the Great North Swim. I was hooked. Not only by swimming but also by the joyful swim community in Clevedon and beyond. As I swam through my first winter, I realised I had more than reclaimed myself; I had found my 'thing', made lasting friendships and boosted my mental health. I now coach all year round. My focus is on helping people discover the mental health benefits of outdoor swimming.

SWIM PATCH:
BRISTOL CHANNEL

When you think of the Bristol Channel, you probably think of mud and docklands. But, between Bridgwater Bay's mudflats and the industrial docks of Avonmouth, Clevedon is an outdoor swimmer's gem. It even has a marine lake – a seawater infinity pool – that's accessible all the time. Head into the dynamic city of Bristol and you'll find a swimming oasis in the most unexpected of areas

Clevedon Marine Lake
📍 slug.risen.grants

Clevedon Marine Lake is a human-made tidal pool that first opened in March 1929. A 250-metre-long sea wall separates the lake from the awesome tides in the Bristol Channel, making it a haven for swimmers and dippers. At high tide, the marine lake looks like an infinity pool; swimming to the sea wall and gazing across to Wales is a treat, especially on a clear sunny day or when there's snow on the Welsh hills.

Clevedon Marine Lake

For a couple of days each month the tide is higher than 12.6 metres and tops over the sea wall. While some daring swimmers will dip in the lake when it's topping over, this should be done with great caution because it's hard to see the lake's edges and railings. The tides bring with them silt, which clouds the water. But in between the top-over tides, the silt settles and the water can become clear enough to see the eels that burrow into the mud on the lake bed. If you swim at night, you'll soon realise that this is when the eels are active as they brush against you.

But the most wonderful thing of all about this pool is the vast, friendly swimming community who swims daily here from the deep end closest to the Salthouse pub.

The lake is open 24/7 almost every day of the year. Check the calendar before you go because it's sometimes drained for maintenance. It's maintained by a charity, whose volunteers lovingly litter-pick and clean around it almost every day, so please donate every time you swim. Or why not become a member or volunteer yourself?

Clevedon Pier
◉ composers.decay.lamp

With one of the highest tidal ranges in the world, the push and pull of the sea here always reminds you that you and your problems are titchy-small. A sea swim under Clevedon's iconic pier is challenging and exciting. The tide is massive, and swimmers emerge from the sea here wearing huge smiles and the infamous Clevedon beard, left there by the water which is brown with silt.

Clevedon's swimming tradition dates back to Victorian times. At high tide most days, swimmers, some of whom are well into their eighties, dip here, swimming 'twelve strokes out and twelve strokes back'. They have their own cave in the sea wall where they change, and they've been the subject of films and documentaries. The 'other cave' is where everybody else changes, and here you'll find swimmers of all shapes and sizes, some of whom dip in the bay where the current is least strong, while others will swim to and from Ladye Bay or around the pier.

Swimming under the Grade I listed pier, which Sir John Betjeman called 'the most beautiful pier in England', is quite an experience. But it's not for the faint-hearted. It's worth remembering that this is an estuary, so you don't just have to consider the tide pushing and pulling to the beach, but also the flow up and down the Channel. This current gets stronger as the tide goes out; so strong, in fact, that even the most capable swimmers would struggle to swim against it. This, and the mudflats left behind as the tide recedes, is why you must only swim half-an-hour

River Avon

either side of high tide. You should start your swim against the current so that it helps you on your return leg and not venture out further than the second or third pier leg if the water is rough.

River Avon, Eastwood Farm
📍 stays.little.rushed

Among industrial estates and residential streets in this south-eastern area of Bristol, you'll find an oasis. At the end of a cul-de-sac, a gravel track winds down through the woods to a café called Beeses Riverside Bar. There's a small car park there, or you can park at the top and walk down. Just to the right of Beeses, you'll find Eastwood Farm nature reserve, and this is where you can swim. The river is wide and its current lazy. It's just a question of wandering along the bank looking for a suitable access point between the grass and shrubs.

On hot summer days, Eastwood Farm takes on the feel of a festival and can get very busy. You can avoid the crowds by walking further along the bank. In high season, stay close to the bank, wear a bright swim hat and tow float and watch out for watercraft. During wetter weather, the bank can be very muddy. A pair of water shoes might be a good idea for navigating slippery banks. As with all rivers, avoid swimming after heavy rains.

It's a nature reserve – with all manner of wildlife and waterfowl – so considerate use is paramount. Park with thought to local residents, or get the number 1 bus to Broomhill Road.

RUTH DOWN,
North Devon
GP
📷 DEVONSWIMGIRLS

I have always loved the outdoors but only started wild swimming five years ago. It has added a whole new dimension, a true immersion in nature and a wonderful way to leave the worries of everyday life behind.

SWIM PATCH:
NORTH DEVON

The North Devon coastline is absolutely stunning with its sandy coves, spectacular cliffs and wild moorland. There's something for everyone, whether you want the classic seaside holiday or something more adventurous. There are some busy beaches but plenty of hidden gems too.

Lee Bay
📍 **pocket.aquatic.exits**

Down a narrow lane lined with fuchsia hedges, a last-minute turn reveals a beautiful rocky bay, with no sand at high tide but plenty of sandy coves at low tide. It's great for exploring rock pools and swimming in long gullies formed by the vertical rock strata which make North Devon's geology so unique. If you're lucky, you'll see a seal! Lee Bay is on the coastal path and the Lee Abbey estate; a toilet and tea cottage are open from May to September.

Barricane Beach
📍 **wooden.starfish.issues**

On the edge of the seaside town of Woolacombe, this is a narrow beach famous for its millions of shells, including cowries and other exotic species, locally rumoured to have washed across from the Caribbean, with the bonus of plenty of deep jumpable rock pools at low tide. Barricane Beach Café is loved for its Sri Lankan curries – but it's only there in the summer because a crane hoists it away to keep it safe from the winter storms!

Northam Burrows
📍 **daydream.guides.whispers**

Drive down through Northam and through the golf course to park at Sandymere.

There you will find the ultimate beginner's sea swimming beach: when the tide is mid or low, there are acres of gently shelving sand, with no significant rips. (However, you will sometimes find you are gently pulled along parallel to the beach.) At high tide the water will reach the pebble ridge and it can be tricky entering or leaving, but at all other times it is very safe. There's an RNLI lifeguard in season. It's all very family friendly, and the famous local Hockings ice cream from the van is highly recommended. Enjoy spectacular views across Bideford Bay to Clovelly and out towards Lundy Island.

SWIM FEELING

All my worries have washed away and nature has rushed in to fill the gap.

RHIANNON STARKS,
Devon
GP & enjoyer of the simple things in life
DEVONSWIMGIRLS

Ruth and I met in 2012, never imagining we'd be the best of swim friends! Ruth grew up playing in the streams of the New Forest, while I spent my childhood dipping with my grandmother in South Devon. Devonswimgirls was born in 2018 after I merrily told everyone on my wedding day how I had skinny dipped in Foggintor Quarry that morning. A little while later Ruth asked me if she could join me skinny dipping and the rest is history. We spend most of our swimming time together on Dartmoor, with the occasional coastal adventure.

SWIM PATCH:
DARTMOOR

The magic of Dartmoor is hard to describe until you set foot there; the vastness, the ability to get away from civilisation and not see a soul, the history, the flora and fauna, the weathered granite tors – and the absolutely unpredictable fog, rain, hail and glorious sunshine. The moor spoils you for swim spots, ranging from small dipping holes, huge lakes, granite quarries, waterfalls, peat cuttings, rivers and streams.

Foggintor Quarry
📍 surpasses.animal.makeovers

This dramatic jagged cleft in the moorland was one of three granite quarries on Dartmoor from the early 1800s. It provided the granite for Nelson's Column, as well as Princetown and Dartmoor Prison. It is almost hidden and the chasm can cause a gasp of surprise if approached over the moorland from nearby North Hessary Tor. The water is calm and clear, except on windy days when the surface is striped with ripples and spray. There are several routes in, but our preferred entry is to approach from the northeast (an easy scramble up a slope from the track further along towards Princetown), where a small steep path hugs the edge of the quarry (not for the faint-hearted; good shoes are needed) and takes you down into the bottom.

If you follow the track and aim for the edge of the water you will find a large rock wall with a shallow pool which leads into the main quarry. Here the entrance is flatter and easier and the quarry gently shelves away. Be aware, though, that the quarry gets quite shallow again in the middle, near the islands of reeds.

The quarry is popular with visitors and campers in the height of summer. We have been surprised (without swimsuits!) by the army climbing on the rock faces above us, and once by a helicopter flying over filming for a Bear Grylls survival course.

For refreshments, Fox Tor Café in nearby Princetown is cosy, does great breakfasts and welcomes dogs. Eversfield Organic Dartmoor Inn at Merrivale has a lovely little shed serving hot drinks and cakes, plus a friendly goat who wears a hi-vis jacket to keep warm in winter.

Crazywell Pool
📍 dwell.moons.lawfully

A large moorland pool, hidden in the swathes of blowing grasses and curves of the landscape. It is approximately 100 metres long and is thought to be either a flooded mineshaft or a reservoir. As it is maintained by a spring, the water level is fairly constant except in very hot, dry weather, and it makes for a good swim spot when the rivers are swollen and unsafe to swim in. A restored old granite cross nearby probably marked a track used by monks across the moor.

There are many legends about Crazywell Pool. It was once, for instance, believed to be bottomless (its maximum depth is just under five metres at the western end). It's also said that at dusk it calls out the name of the next parishioner to die. Nonetheless, we have had many a safe and delightful swim here! The easiest entry is via a natural beach at the south end, which is gentle and fairly smooth.

The pool itself can be approached either from Princetown, via some well-maintained paths, the Devonport Leat, or from Norsworthy Bridge at the edge of Burrator Reservoir, where there is a track going up along the edge of the Norsworthy plantation and onto the open moor. We recommend an OS map for this swim, as the pool itself is off the beaten track and can be difficult to find, especially in the fog Dartmoor is so prone to.

Cadover Bridge

Fogginter Quarry

River Plym, Cadover Bridge
📍 scared.blacken.spires

This area provides a wealth of dips, swim spots and paddling for all ages and abilities, though it's often busy in the holidays. There is a car park (often frequented by an ice cream van) and a wide grassy area next to the river for picnics.

For a wonderful deep swim we recommend following the path downstream from the bridge through the green mossy woodland. An old clay pipe lines the floor of the path. Now largely broken, it used to transport liquid China clay. It leads to a spot which is nice for a shallow dip and back jacuzzi. Continue further along the pipe path, through a fence and little bridge until you see a small track coming up from the river on the right. Follow this down to a deep waterfall pool with a rope swing, and a small cliff where you can jump safely depending on the water levels. At one end you will see a nice shallow slope into the pool, where it is easy to get in. It can be a bit slippery at the final descent to the pool so good shoes are recommended.

JOANNE CLEMENT & FAMILY,
Porthleven, Cornwall
Elopement photographers
🌐 CORNWALL-ELOPEMENTS.CO.UK

We are a little family living in Porthleven, Cornwall. I am originally from South Africa, where swimming was a huge part of growing up. After moving to Ireland, I then ran away from home to the UK, then finally to Cornwall to study marine photography and film. I fell pregnant in my third year of university and Keynvor (whose name means 'Ocean' in Cornish) has been exhausting me ever since!

Two years ago I met my partner Patrick who was visiting from Germany and introduced him to this wonderful new sea world. We are super laidback and don't take life too seriously. Most days we can be found outside – hiking the coast path, eating cream teas on the cliffs and finding hidden swim spots for wild skinny dips. Keynvor loves looking for high cliffs to jump off into deep rock pools. We are currently trying to walk the entire Cornish coastline at low tide to find secret coves and rock pools for wild swimming.

SWIM PATCH:
CORNWALL

Cornwall has one of the most stunning coastlines in the UK. At over 400 miles long, there is so much choice, from white sandy beaches to hidden rocky coves. The weather is also much milder than elsewhere in the UK, making it easier for winter swimming as a family and staying in a little longer. There is an abundance of marine life and we often see seals and dolphins.

In the winter we tend to use rock pools or tidal pools – there are many left behind by the miners from the mining period and these are often such great finds. Many of them were blown out with dynamite, but they look so natural. They are very deep and wide and often higher up on the cliffs, allowing you to swim easily for two or three hours before low tide, giving you a longer swimming window.

Trescore Islands
messy.roosters.glad

It is best to park at Park Head and walk down the coastal path, through a little wooded valley passing by another great swimming spot called Porth Mear Cove. Or park at Porthcothan and Bedruthan Steps if you want to take in more of the coast path first, with its stunning views over the ocean. Bring some goggles, as these coves are often filled with sea kelp and marine life and the visibility is amazing. This is a great high tide and low tide spot on really calm days. If it is calm you can swim across to the islands to explore the rocky outcrops and sea caves.

There is no offcial path that I have seen, but more of a climb down the rocks at the front and onto the rocky beach or gullies on the left-hand side. There are lots of rock pools to explore too. It is great for kids and families who feel comfortable climbing.

Porthcothan
softest.crackling.mixture

Close to Trescore Islands, but the more accessible of the two, with toilets and a café and no need for climbing over rocks to get onto the beach. This makes it much busier than Trescore Islands, so best to go earlier in the day to avoid crowds. We aim to swim before 10 a.m. during the height of the summer season. The best time to go is the one to two hours before low tide so you can access the hidden gullies, rock pools and shifting sand pools hidden between the rocks. Be careful if swimming in the sea as there are two known powerful rips at low and high tide. When there is no lifeguard cover, we prefer to swim in the gullies that are sheltered and the natural sea pools. Head down to the right-hand side of the beach to find our favourite swimming spots.

There is a good sized car park for this beach and a little café called Porthcothan Bay Stores, which sells lovely homemade soups, pasties, hot drinks and ice cream for after your swim.

Nanjizal Beach
whizzed.sticky.inflating

Park at Land's End and walk for about half an hour along the coast path towards this magical, sheltered bay. It is best to swim here one to two hours before low tide so

Porthcothan

you can access the sea cave and swim in the sea pool. We recommend visiting early in the morning or later in the day if you want to swim alone. However, if the pool is busy the sea is just as lovely and clear on a calm day and seals often frequent the bay. The sand levels change here quite dramatically and can make the pool deeper or shallower. The sand seems to be returning slowly to the cove after most of it was washed away. It's a good spot for seal watching, particularly round the corner at Zawn Reeth.

Housel Bay
◊ nosedive.mango.lyrics

We love this little beach. Best to park at the Lizard and walk the 10 to 15 minutes across the fields, as there is no parking in the hotel above the cove, unless you are a guest. You will need to clamber across some big boulders to reach the sand but it's worth the effort for a quieter beach with amazing views, sea caves and clear seas for a sheltered swim in paradise. In the winter we have never seen other people on the beach so you can skinny dip in the off season if you are feeling brave, but please be aware that this beach can become cut off at higher tides, so be careful. This beach, on mainland Britain's most southerly point, is relatively sheltered, as the high cliffs also provide cover from the wind.

Prussia Cove
📍 **woodstove.garlic.face**

We love this little section of coastline, with its hidden coves, sheltered bays and rich history. Secluded and romantic, Prussia Cove has an olde-worlde poetic feel. It is famous as being the home of the Carter family of 18th-century smugglers – one of whom, Harry Carter, became known as the King of Prussia. There are long walks around here and it's great for swimming off the rocks and for enjoying sunset picnics.

The car park only holds about eight cars, so arrive early to avoid disappointment. The public road leading down to it is very narrow, with passing places here and there (I am always thankful when I make it down without another car coming in the other direction). There are no facilities. The coves are at least a 10-minute walk from the car park, but space and access to these depends on the tide. Dogs are allowed all year round.

Fisherman's Cove

LAURA EVANS,
St Ives
Outdoor tour guide
📷 STIVESMERMAID

I've been a passionate year-round outdoor swimmer for seven years and there isn't a day that I'm not grateful for the simple, rewarding joy of immersing myself in the water. Outdoor swimming always brings me back to myself – and has taught me a strength and a resilience I didn't know I had. It has brought me the most magical experiences and introduced incredible people into my life.

I can't really talk about my swim journey without mentioning the fact that I also have a fully functioning mermaid tail and am known to many as the St Ives Mermaid. For six years I have washed up on the beaches around St Ives to meet and greet children (and adults!), making St Ives the first seaside town with its own resident mermaid.

SWIM PATCH:
CORNWALL

I often describe Cornwall as the most enchanting playground for those who love the outdoors. Whether you want the rugged coast or wild moorland, a secluded beach or raging waves, we have it all. I grew up swimming in the Cornish water and I have an indescribably deep connection with the landscape here. The coastline is studded with old mine ruins. You can find spots that once would have been frequented by tin miners and so you are truly swimming and immersing yourself in the history and heritage of the area.

Porthtowan Tidal Pool
📍 slippery.plants.amplifier

A mermaid pool if ever there was one! Nestled right under towering cliffs, accessible over rocks (so wear sensible shoes) at low tide this is a beautiful turquoise manmade tidal infinity pool. Accessible only at low tide, so make sure you check before you head out. (I use My Tide Times.) Parking available, but it can be limited during busy periods so, as ever, the earlier you can go the better.

Boat Cove, Pendeen
📍 winters.rumble.skies

Want to swim in a pool blasted into the rocks by the famous Cornish tin miners? Yes, really! They used dynamite to blast these unique swimming spots into the cliffs near to where they worked. And now it's the perfect way to refresh after a long walk along the southwest coast path. Again, it's accessible only at low tide.

If you want a truly magical experience then I suggest heading there at sunrise and watching the light shift and change as you float in the water. You're pretty much guaranteed to have them to yourself if you go early as well.

Cape Cornwall Tidal Pool
📍 dolphins.hobbies.sized

Another infinity tidal pool, this time sheltering in the rocks below the famous Cape in Priest Cove. Take underwater photos in the dazzlingly clear water or lie on the edge watching the wild sea rip around the Brison's (an islet that looks like a man lying in a bath tub). Accessible only at low tide, and with parking that is often busy.

Boat Cove

Freshwater Bay

MADI DEW,
Isle of Wight
Learning support assistant
DIPPINGSOCIETY

I grew up on the Isle of Wight, so being in the sea has always been a huge part of my life, but after the loss of a friend 2018, I decided to challenge myself to wild swim every day for a year. It wasn't quite so popular then and lots of locals were interested in what we (my friend Kim and I) were doing and asking if they could join us, as we looked like we were having the time of our lives. And so the Dipping Society was founded.

SWIM PATCH:
ISLE OF WIGHT

The Isle of Wight is a pretty special place, especially when it comes to the sea. We are very lucky to be diamond-shaped, so basically whatever the wind direction or weather there is generally a nice sheltered spot to jump in the sea. The tide can be an issue, with strong currents in some places and access a bit more difficult at low tide. Even in the summer when all the tourists descend from the mainland you can still find empty beaches.

Gurnard Bay
woke.unicorns.helpfully

Gurnard is situated about a mile along the coast from the sailing town of Cowes, where the RedJet arrives from Southampton. It's a nice, flat stroll along the seafront and when you encounter the iconic green beach huts you've made it to your destination. You are not met by miles

Osbourne Bay

of golden sand, but rather about 50 yards of rocky, occasionally seaweedy coastline, which regardless of preconceptions is, for so many, an absolute slice of paradise. I think because it's not your typical 'day out on the beach' that it retains a bit of charm that mostly locals appreciate. Plus, it's never too busy – well, not until Sundays at 9 a.m. when our stoic group of dippers meets for our weekly social swim. All are welcome!

Watch out for strong tides, it's sometimes like a swimming treadmill. Low tide can make entry difficult, so have some shoes to wear to walk across the beach. At high tide the sea can be accessed via public slipway for those with mobility issues, although it can be quite slippery. Go up into the village to the Gurnard Press for a coffee and cake or a pizza after.

Gurnard Bay

Freshwater Bay
◉ flamed.accordion.machine

'The Bay', as it's known by locals, is a sight to behold, with Mermaid Rock on one side and secret smugglers' tunnels on the other, and a house teetering ominously close to the edge of the brilliant white cliffs. The beach is made up of shingle and large pebbles, so no pesky sand to get out of all your crevices after a day here! The beach shelves quickly into the sea, so it makes for a quick entry but a rather undignified exit. The water is crystal clear in the summer and, if you bring your goggles, you'll probably meet some of our aquatic residents. Watch out for big swell here: often it is not safe to swim as there can be a big shore break. For some delicious food and coffee (oh, and it also serves beer!), head up the road to the Piano Café, where you can sit with a view over Tennyson Down.

Osbourne Bay
◉ perfect.forensic.rave

This 'secret' beach is accessible only through Osbourne House, for a fee or free if you have English Heritage membership. A hidden gem, which only opened

Gurnard Bay

to the public a few years ago, it's a long walk from the house (Queen Victoria's old holiday home), but if you're lucky you could see ten different species of butterfly on your way down.

For those who don't fancy a walk, there is a free shuttle bus that runs down to the beach at regular intervals (check for seasonal times). It is mostly sandy, but like a lot of the beaches on the island the sand gets shifted around after a big storm. Osbourne Bay is a special area of conservation and is home to seagrass beds, which act as protection for breeding seahorses. There can be a strong tide here even when the water looks seemingly calm.

POST SWIM SNACK

One of Katie's famous cakes. Katie started swimming with us back in 2018 and her baking skills have become as popular as the group itself! When pandemic rules allow, we always have tea or coffee (provided by my mum) and cake at the beach huts after our Sunday morning swim. We put a pot out and collect donations for local mental health charities in return.

River Wye

OH, THE PLACES YOU'LL GO!

IN WALES

Pobbles Beach

ALISON OWEN,
Gower

Ex-teacher, now full-time family administrator, manager & herder

GOWERMERMATES

In 2018, after 25 years of teaching and juggling life with three daughters, one of whom has profound, multiple disabilities, I hit the mid-life wall . . . hard. My GP diagnosed 'depression and anxiety', until I pointed out that I was bloody homicidal, and certainly not depressed, after which he diagnosed the perimenopause. I eventually finished work to focus on the admin and battles that come with disability services, and to learn to slow down and breathe.

Living in Gower and being so close to the sea and beaches that I had not had time to enjoy for so long, in September 2018 I decided to learn to surf in my spare time. I soon gave up on the board and the wetsuit to simply play in the waves in my swimsuit. A friend started joining me and, for the first year, we were very much dippers, splashing in waves but not really swimming any great distances. Over time we began swimming a little further.

Sgwd y Pannwr

SWIM PATCH:
THE GOWER PENINSULA

The UK's first area of outstanding natural beauty, this peninsula is only 19 miles long but packs in a varied landscape – cliffs, woodlands, salt marshes, moorland and some star beaches, including Rhossili/Llangennith and Three Cliffs.

Several are well-known surf beaches. Jumping over or diving under the rollers is the best way to bring out our inner daredevils and reminds us of who we used to be, before jobs, mortgages and families made us all sensible! Other beaches are flatter, ideal for swimming, sometimes a gentle chatty breaststroke and sometimes a heads-down front crawl. Gower's AONB designation means that tourist development is limited, but therein lies its beauty: quiet country pubs, cafés with homemade cakes, a couple of farm shops are all mostly off the beaten track rather than part of an established tourist industry.

Port Eynon

Port Eynon to Horton
◉ leathers.connected.latter

This lovely kilometre-ish cross-the-bay swim can be done in either direction and isn't crowded out by the jet skis and SUPs that tend to use Oxwich. Try to avoid mid to low tide at Port Eynon as the rocks can be a literal pain. Horton is a better bet if the tide is out and is always quieter than Port Eynon in midsummer. The remains of oyster pools and an old harbour wall are visible at low tide and to the right of the bay is the 18th-century Salt House ruin – extracting sea salt was possibly a cover for smuggling!

There are a few popular chip shops but if you walk 50 metres further you'll find the Coffee House, serving homemade cakes by Rosehip Bakes. Zoë bakes fresh every day; her brownies are not to be missed.

Langland Beach
◉ vaccines.crackled.restriction

This is a winter favourite, best done at sunrise, when the early morning cold means this popular beach is quiet. Check the surf first and aim for the middle of the bay to avoid the drag that can pull you out towards the right side of the bay. A Champagne breakfast at the Langland Brasserie is a real treat, while hot chocolate and cakes at the Surfside café means you can warm up near their real fire. In the summer, Langland is busy, being the closest beach to the village of Mumbles.

At the other end of the day and the other end of Gower, Llangennith/Hillend is perfect for a summer sunset with Worm's Head silhouetted against big skies.

Beware the high-tide rips and enjoy being barrelled by some of Gower's best surf.

Pobbles Beach
📍 glows.payout.title

This beach is next to the iconic Three Cliffs Bay, but generally offers a much safer swim. Getting there requires a bit of a walk across the clifftops from the car park (gladiators.model.microchip) and down through the dunes, but it's definitely worth it. Park at the National Trust Southgate car park and walk west and you'll see castle ruins, a valley that fills with water at high tide and dramatic cliffs on your wander down. In the summer nights, this is a great little bay for swimming, with bioluminescent plankton and the Milky Way above, but it's pitch black so make sure you go with someone who knows the route!

> ### WARM UP TIP
> Laughter. My local group, the Gower Mermates, can make sailors blush and innuendo bingo works every time.

Llangennith

Llyn y Fan Fach

LAURA TRUELOVE,
Swansea
Digital content creator
◉ WILDSWIMWALES

As a surfer, I'd always been scared of swimming. Going in the sea without my board, I felt naked and vulnerable, stripped of my lifeline in a mass of water. My journey is one of overcoming that fear, or thalassophobia. It has now spread from oceans into lakes and rivers, and slowly but surely I'm growing accustomed to swimming in places I know are home to weird, wild and sometimes scary underwater life. It started with some friends coaxing me in and then I kept going back for more. Now I can't get enough of that post-swim tingle.

The summer sunshine on my face as I immerse myself feels divine, but there's something a little more special about the winter. There's that determination and reward when it's colder. They say 'only a surfer knows the feeling' and this refers to the high of surfing a wave. But there's a high to be had with cold water swimming, too; a numbing sort of high. I guess that's why we keep coming back for more, no matter how cold.

SWIM PATCH:
SOUTH WALES

There's so much for the swimmer here, from the lakes of the Brecon Beacons to long, sand-dune beaches, plus a vibrant wild swim community to embrace you.

Merthyr Mawr
◉ fittingly.proof.nozzles

A really big beach backed by dramatic dunes that include Europe's second largest: at 61 metres, it's called the Big Dipper. Best reached after parking at the car park behind the dunes (ember.weeks.taller) and taking the 30-minute walk through them. It's also possible to park at Ogmore-by-Sea and cross the sands, but only when the tide is out. Be careful of tidal movements as this is a small estuary.

This is a beach I loved exploring when I was living in Cardiff. People ride horses here and there's a wave that breaks in the estuary mouth, so you'll find surfers here too. Welsh rugby players train by running up and down the dune. The car park gets quite full on a busy day, but lots of people tend to go to Ogmore because it's a shorter walk. Parking is cheap, a few pounds for the day, and there's often a little horsebox van with snacks, drinks and coffee.

Rotherslade
◉ giants.whisk.spots

This very small beach is one with a vibrant community. It was here that Rachel Ashe started Mental Health Swims, and the group still meets regularly there (follow on Instagram or Facebook and look for the pink pirate flag on the beach). This is a small inlet, with a pebble beach that is entirely consumed at high tide, but pretty, with lovely steps leading to it, as if it were a theatre. When it's sunny it's nice to simply sit up on them and dry off. There's also the Surfside café, which does lovely coffees. Only one street leads down to it and it's hard to park on a nice day, but it's connected to the coast path, so you can to go for a run all the way along the Gower and end up at this beach for a swim.

Ten minutes away is the popular surfers' beach of Langland Bay. Along that coastline you have so many options, but the reason I say Rotherslade specifically is because of the community.

Llyn y Fan Fawr, Brecon Beacons
◉ front.gymnasium.snapped

I first went here with Queens of Antur (Welsh for 'adventure'). It's one of two lakes, Llyn y Fan Fawr and Llyn y Fan Fach, around which there is all kinds of folklore – and there is so much Welsh folklore. It's worth reading Horatio Clare's *Brecon Beacons Myths & Legends*. Llyn y Fan Fach is the site of the Arthurian Lady of the Lake.

POST SWIM DRINK

Rum. Welsh Barti Ddu rum. It's just beautiful. I bought a hip flask and some steel cups and I take them with me and we'll have a tot after. It really warms you up! I've also invested in a little portable burner and cafetière. Yes, flasks take up less space and are less hassle, but nothing beats a fresh coffee . . . and why not add a tot of rum while you're at it?! (It goes without saying, don't drive afterwards.)

Rotherslade

Start your walk to the lake(s) opposite Tafarn y Garreg (pelting.winks.twee). It has a car park or you can park further up the lane. Be mindful of the wild sheep, but if you're up for a long walk you can do both Llyn y Fan Fawr and Llyn y Fan Fach. There are plenty of deep pools and mini waterfalls in the Tawe here. I've heard rumours of eels, so watch your toes – I recommend boots! As you dip, look out for red kites, which are beautiful to see soaring above you. The Tafarn y Garreg ('Stone Pub'), is a lovely little inn which serves wonderful Welsh pale ales – perfect at the end of a long day.

ESSENTIAL KIT

This is a surfer tip. Take a big plastic gardening bucket with handles, one you can put all your wet stuff in but big enough to stand in too. I put my dryrobe on and I get undressed in the bucket. And I'll also take a hot water bottle and if my feet get really cold I empty it in the bucket, so my feet are standing in this lovely warm water.

Blue Pool

RACHEL ASHE,
Swansea
Founder of Mental Health Swims
🌐 MENTALHEALTHSWIMS.CO.UK

I am an adopted, mixed race, plus-size, queer woman with one of the most stigmatised mental illnesses out there. I have spent a lot of my life feeling like I don't fit in. It's only since taking up swimming outdoors that I have realised that maybe not fitting in could be a strength rather than a weakness.

I started my cold-water journey on New Year's Day in 2019 at the Loony Dook in Edinburgh. The experience was life changing. I was really unwell at the time, the kind of unwell where you have medication to get you through the day and medication to get you through the night. I think the bitter cold helped me remember I'm alive and that I wanted to fight to get better. It's not a miracle cure and I'll probably always have to take medication. But cold water gives me a much-needed boost to be able to manage my symptoms in as healthy a way as possible.

I set up Mental Health Swims to try and make it easier for people living with mental health challenges to feel confident about joining a group of people they haven't met before. We try and remove as many of the barriers as we can to make this possible. Our aim is to make welcoming, inclusive spaces so more people can enjoy the benefits of cold water and community.

SWIM PATCH:
SWANSEA

I live in Swansea, which means I am on the doorstep of the Gower Peninsula, a designated area of outstanding natural beauty. There are incredible beaches all the way round the coastline and each one is special in its own way. Water is a vital part of our life here and as a family we spend a huge amount of time in or near water.

Pwll Du
📍 tuxedos.duck.habits

This beach never gets too busy because there are no parking or facilities nearby. You need to park up and then walk for about quarter of an hour to get there. It is a pretty cove with a few houses nestled at the back surrounded by trees. I always spend a large portion of time at Pwll Du imagining living in the large white house at the back! I love the rock formations around the bay; they offer pockets of privacy so you can change into your swimming costume. The stones on this beach fascinate me: they are grey with white stripes like many of the stones around Gower but on this beach the lines are thicker compared with the lines on the stones just a few bays further along the coast. I find myself wondering, why is that?

Blue Pool, near Broughton Bay
📍 **lump.begun.driftwood**

This spot can get busy so it's worth going very early in the morning at low tide so you can walk from Broughton Bay rather than scrambling down from the headland. It's a tidal pool which is almost perfectly round and very deep. It gets fully submerged at high tide. It is a beautiful, secluded beach; when you're lucky enough to be there alone it feels wonderfully peaceful. I love the nooks and crannies for setting up camp for a few hours. We bring the Kelly kettle and lots of picnic things and enjoy jumping into the pool from the sides.

Bracelet Bay
📍 **hunk.legs.quilt**

Right in the Mumbles, around the corner from the pier; is my favourite beach. We call it Moominland because that's what it feels like. It's a pebbly beach with little rocky coves and a lighthouse. It's the best place for leaning against the rocks and drying off in the sunshine.

For a post-swim feed, there is an amazing fish and chip shop on Mumbles pier called Copper Fish. They do delicious minty mushy peas. And on the seafront in Mumbles there are also now some brilliant food huts including the Shared Plate and the Gower Seafood Hut.

POST SWIM WARM UP

Have a cuddle.

MARK HARVEY,
Forest of Dean & Wye Valley
Timetabling education officer
WYE NOT SWIM? A COMMUNITY SWIM GROUP

My first dip in open water was in spring 2019 in the River Wye. To be honest, I wasn't much of a swimmer. I was a regular marathon runner until injury brought my running career to a sudden halt. Running was my stress and anxiety buster, and when it went I soon got fat, unfit and very fed up.

Seeing my desperate state and worried for my sanity, my wife set me the challenge of swimming the Diabetes 22 charity event. And just to make it a little more difficult, she dared me to do it outside in open water. As an experienced open water swimmer, she knew the mental and physical benefits open water swimming would gift me.

After that first dip in the Wye I was hooked. Swimming in open water became my therapy to life's challenges.

SWIM PATCH:
FOREST OF DEAN & WYE VALLEY

What makes this area so special is the number and variety of swims available to outdoor swim enthusiasts. Right on our doorstep we have three rivers – the Wye, the Usk and the Monnow – and the lakes in the Brecons. A short journey away is the fabulous Bathurst Lido, and just over the Severn is Clevedon Marine Lake and the Clevedon beaches.

River Wye from Dixton Church to Monmouth Rowing Club
- beast.series.birdcage (car park)
- topical.goals.staining (entry point)

This is where I took my first-ever swim, and a group of us meet regularly here. You have two options: either park at Monmouth Rowing Club and walk upriver to St Peter's Church at Dixton and then swim back down to the club, about a kilometre each way. Or park by the church in Dixton Lane and do it the other way round. If the river is running particularly quickly it's almost a swoosh

Monmouth Rowing Club

back downriver, so you can do it more than once. If you prefer, there's a wooden pontoon about 800 metres upstream from the rowing club which gives easy access to the river. Exit using the steps just before the Wye River Bridge.

Entry into the river at Dixton Church is by the steps in the churchyard, where in days gone by a ferry used to land when it brought the church's attendees from upriver. It's so peaceful in the churchyard and it's a great place from which to launch yourself gently into the river for your swim or float back downstream.

The river here is reasonably safe. But the rowing club is popular and can be busy; call them to check events if you're travelling long distance.

River Wye from Goodrich Castle to Kerne Bridge
📍 blogging.stages.sour

This is a lovely swim along a peaceful and tranquil stretch of the Wye. Park on or alongside the bridge after which the small hamlet of Kerne Bridge is named (where the B4229 meets the B4234, and near the Inn on the Wye).

Follow the public footpath back upstream on the left riverbank (the river to your right). The impressive building up on the hill as you walk along is Goodrich Castle, dating back to the Norman Conquest. After about a mile the footpath runs into a wooded area (powder.cheese. simmer) and it's here that you access the river. It's an easy scramble down the bank to the river, and a paddle out into the middle, where the river drops off to become swimmable. The choice is then a lazy float or a gentle swim back to Kerne Bridge.

You have several options for exiting the river. You can walk out of the water onto the riverbank on the right about 20 metres upriver from the bridge, or swim under the bridge to exit just before the river becomes swifter across some shallow rapids. Or, if you're feeling brave, you can scramble across the rapids (staying in the water) and then swim on another 400 metres to exit at the canoe launch on the left. It's then a short walk back along the public footpath to Kerne Bridge.

The longer swim through the shallow rapids isn't one to try if the river is in fast flow as you can easily be dragged across. Also, on a warm summer's day, the launch can be incredibly busy, so exiting there may involve dodging families afloat in various river-going vessels.

River Monnow, Skenfrith Castle
spotty.croaking.voted

Though it's more of a dip than a swim, this is one of my absolute favourites! Skenfrith is quite remote, but it's well worth the effort to find it just for the joy of swimming in the grounds of a medieval castle and knowing that people have been using the river here for literally hundreds of years.

Park in the castle car park and it's a short walk to the river. The best way to do this is to enter the grounds of the castle itself (up a set of wooden steps) and walk out through the medieval gateway to the river. A few hundred metres along the riverbank towards the deserted watermill you'll find what looks like a small sandy beach. Enter here – there's a gentle slope and then a sudden drop-off, so just ten metres from the beach you can't touch the bottom.

Swim against the current keeping to the left of the river and head up towards the rapids: watch out for large rocks before them. If you're brave you can launch yourself into the water just before the rapids and swoosh back downriver to the start. The river becomes very shallow as you pass the beach entry point, serving as a natural stopping place. Don't be tempted to swim down to the bridge as the river is full of washed-down rocks and bits of trees.

For fitter swimmers, there is the opportunity to swim in an infinity pool just before the rapids – no matter how hard you swim, you stay in the same place. Or, if you're like me, you suddenly give up and swoosh back down the river giggling like a three-year-old.

Llyn Mymbyr

Cardigan Bay, near Mwnt

TANYA KNIGHT,
Carmarthenshire
College lecturer
HAPPYWELSHFEET

I'm lucky enough to be approaching my half-century and I have the wrinkles, stress and laughter lines to prove it. I've worked in education for over twenty years and I love teaching. Most working days feel like a whirlwind of lessons, paperwork and dealing with student issues so self-care is a priority. The feeling of exhilaration followed by contentment that a cold swim brings means that wild swimming has become an increasingly important part of my life.

Living near the coast is a blessing and, as wild swimming became a regular occurrence, many others became curious about the benefits of cold water therapy. This led to my good friend 'Scottish Anne' and me starting a Bluetits Chill Swimmers group. We are a fully inclusive group of bluetits and bluebells and we meet every Sunday at high tide.

SWIM PATCH:
CARMARTHENSHIRE

The Blue Lagoon
excellent.bunny.raced

A slate quarry until 1910 when it was abandoned and flooded, the lagoon is known for its clear blue water and for hosting the Red Bull Cliff Diving world series. It's safe to say that the water is very deep and very cold! The area is popular with kayakers, SUPers and coasteering enthusiasts, so there's something for everyone. The downside is that it can get busy. If, like me, you like to avoid the crowds then sunrise or sunset is a perfect time to visit for a dip. As the lagoon is so deep you don't need to worry too much about high and low tides.

Another bonus is that it's a short walk from the car park at Abereiddy (local charges apply). If you want to combine it with a coastal walk then why not park in the fishing village of Porthgain. The stunning walk (about 2.3 miles) along the Pembrokeshire coastal path will take you directly to Abereiddy and the Blue Lagoon. Here you'll pass a sandy cove called Traeth Llyfn (Step Beach), only accessible via steep steps from the coastal path. Perfect for a secluded dip.

Porthgain is lovely, with amazing locally caught fish and chips at The Shed. There's also good beer and bar food at the Sloop Inn.

Broad Haven, Nolton Haven & Little Haven
📍 glows.herds.only

Broad Haven is an accessible beach which has a large car park and toilet facilities, as well as lifeguards in high season. (You've also got pubs, a post office, shops and watersports.) Again, the beach can be popular with surfers, SUPers and kayakers.

The reason I love this spot so much is because of the amazing coastal path. If you want to take yourself away from the Blue Flag sheltered golden sandy beach of Broad Haven in search of more secluded spots then head along the coastal path from Broad Haven to Druidstone or even Newgale (if you're feeling adventurous).

Here you'll find quieter, secluded coves and beaches which can only be reached via the coastal path. My favourite is Haroldston Bridge (sometimes known as Devil's Bridge). This is not for the faint-hearted as the scramble from the path down and back is challenging, but you will be rewarded with crystal clear turquoise water on a sunny day. Absolutely stunning!

Mwnt Beach
📍 mermaids.seaweed.caged

This place holds a special place in my heart. So many childhood memories of days spent here on the beach and climbing the cliffs adjacent to spot local dolphins, porpoises and seals.

Mwnt is a beautiful, secluded bay with a sandy beach. There is a National Trust car park (dries.light.morphing), public toilets, a cafe and a tiny white 14th-century church. Quite steep steps lead to the beach, which can get busy during high season. There is no lifeguard service here and the beach is considered relatively safe. However, I have experienced some strong rip tides while swimming here.

The beach faces west, so head to

MICROADVENTURE TIP

There is a path around the whole of the coast of Wales. Think of all the coves, beaches and dipping spots you'll come across by exploring here.

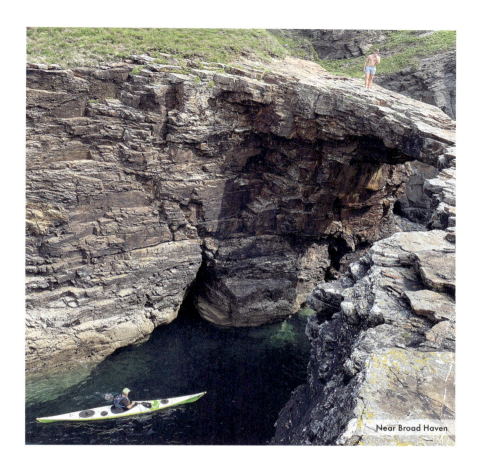

Near Broad Haven

Mwnt later in the evening to avoid the crowds and to catch a stunning sunset. Whether you're after a dip, a wander along the coastal path or a veiw of the sun setting over the sea from the elevated Foel Y Mwnt, this place is magical.

After working up an appetite, head back to Cardigan to Pizzatipi for amazing pizza, salads and craft ales with a view of the River Teifi or pop into Crwst bakery for sandwiches and amazing cakes.

Cwmorthin Quarry

CERI NORTON,
Cwmorthin
Teacher
CEXX12

My love for the outdoors and nature has always been rooted deep within me. When I moved to Liverpool for university, I felt so distant from the mountains and lakes and the rural landscape I'd grown up around. My heart ached to be back. In my mid twenties I started hiking the mountains of Snowdonia, which led me to want to sleep out in the mountains, to wild camp. Eventually, I felt an urge to swim there. I started a challenge to complete 52 Snowdonia swims in the year. Although I didn't quite manage the full 52, I did manage about 45.

SWIM PATCH:
SNOWDONIA

The mountains, lakes, rivers, streams and waterfalls of Snowdonia blow my mind every time. In the water, when you're surrounded by the mountains and floating on your back and looking around, you can feel a part of the place.

Cwmorthin Quarry
happy.precluded.winds

A swimming spot just outside Blaenau Ffestiniog to which my boyfriend took me while we were dating. I thought it was amazing. It is a short walk from the car park up a steep hill, and the pool and waterfall are just off the path. It is not secret or secluded, however go at the right time of day and it can feel remote from the rest of the world. The pool is small and deep and the water flows into it from about 10 feet. The quarry and the grey slates surround.

Llyn Geirionydd
knee.universes.vegetable

I first went to swim in this lake on a cold, autumnal day. Road access is via a tricky, winding single-track lane, but once there you're nestled in deep woods. The lake has a walk which you can do all the way around it. To glide through the stillness of the water and see the ripples which reflect the colours on the trees all around

Llyn Llydaw

is a very special experience. The lake is popular with swimmers on Boxing Day and New Year's Day and also with a local outdoor swimming group, Trefriw Drips, who swim there every Sunday morning at nine o'clock.

Llyn Llydaw
📍 luck.butlers.courage

The route to this lake is from the Pen Y Pass parking in Snowdonia, via the Miner's Track to Snowdon. We spent the night sleeping by the lake and in the morning the depth of the water and the colour was magnificent, turquoise blue and crystal clear. It was so cold yet so refreshing and I glided out across the water with Snowdon towering above. The lake is huge and offers a lot of swimming potential!

TIP FOR A NEWBIE

Take your time, go with a friend, control your breath.

A view of Glyder Fawr

Llyn Idwal

TARA LEANNE HALL,
Eryri/Snowdonia
Independent bookshop assistant
TARA_LEANNE_

I work in Browsers Bookshop (Siop Llyfrau Browsers), a great indie bookshop in Porthmadog. I also run a local period project called Cylch Coch (The Red Circle), which tackles period poverty and period taboo. After university I went travelling and worked in rural Nepal for almost a year. I grew up surrounded by hills and mountains, but when I came back to Wales I felt dislocated, with no roots or purpose here. One winter morning I randomly went for a swim in a pool we swam in as children. I felt truly alive for the first time in a while. Swimming outdoors became a part of me, a way to feel, to challenge myself and to fully appreciate my home's rugged beauty. I love it here, and can't picture myself anywhere else right now.

SWIM PATCH:
ERYRI/SNOWDONIA

A rugged, often ominous, rainy, craggy, wild place full of folklore and myth, where it's possible to swim in deep lakes and fairytale gorge waterfalls hidden in ancient woodland and river pools. I have lived here most of my life and still find new nooks to explore and water to dip into.

Llyn Idwal, Ogwen Valley
tools.rocker.impeached

Necklaced by some very impressive mountains – Y Garn to the right, Y Glyderau in front, Tryfan peeking around the corner to your left and Pen Yr Ole Wen behind on the other side of the Valley. Floating on your back looking up at craggy, uncompromising rock, it's a place you will feel wild. I recommend going in the early morning as it is a popular walking area or, better yet, find a spot to wild camp and wake yourself up with a dip. (Follow the wild-camping code if you do.)

The walk up from the car park at Ogwen Cottage (toilet facilities here), or the handful of laybys as you enter Ogwen Valley, is fairly easy. You may bump into the wild Welsh mountain ponies or wild Welsh mountain goats on your way up. Taking the path to your right as you reach the lake, head over the slate bridge until you reach the beach, a great entrance point. The lake is shallow for a little while, slightly jagged stones underfoot, and then drops off into the cold, deep belly. A well-established path loops around the lake. Weather can change rapidly in the valley, from overcast skies to torrential downpours and gales which send waves crashing against the shore. Be mindful of this and take extra layers and waterproofs.

Watkin Path Pools, Afon Cwn Llan
 colonies.warblers.sleeps

These pools are so much fun! Running alongside the Watkin Path up Yr Wyddfa/Snowdon they can be missed by eager hikers racing to the summit. Wait! Hold up, jump in! Take the Watkin Path from Nant Gwynant also accessible by the S4 bus, which stops at Pont Bethania. As you come to the striking waterfalls on your right, before heading through the gate take the little steep and slippery track down to your right. Skip along the slate bridge and you have arrived at your destination.

Follow the path to the right of the falls and choose the pools you fancy. There are a series of around six good dipping pools: some you can jump into, slide into, climb a rope, even sit behind a waterfall. On a sunny day the water is turquoise but always crisp, especially when there has been snow melt from the top of Snowdon. As they are waterfall pools, make sure the flow is swimmable; the rainfall can turn the pools into cascades.

Make a day of it and carry on up the

Llyn Idwal

path to the summit of Yr Wyddfa/Snowdon. Or, if you would rather head for a warming panad (cuppa), head back down the trail to Caffi Gwynant. Tasty, homemade food and great coffee in a converted chapel.

Cricieth Beach
📍 **words.again.happening**

Snowdonia is where the mountains meet the sea, so you can't leave without dipping your toes into the waters of Cardigan Bay. This beach sits alongside the town of Cricieth, a clutch of multicoloured Victorian houses and ancient castle ruins perched on the craggy headland, destroyed by one of Wales's most powerful medieval princes, Owain Glyndŵr.

The pebbly beaches to both sides of the castle are great spots to enter the water. During high tide at the main beach you can jump off the lower stone jetty. I prefer to stroll up the hill to the castle and descend to the beach on its northerly side. The wooden wave breakers are great to balance and dive off and there is more sense of seclusion.

The wild swimmers @woolly_hatters meet on Cricieth Beach throughout the year and welcome everyone. Public toilets are beside the main beach and car park. Take a stroll up the prom to the RNLI lifeboat station and donate if you can. Look out for the Cariad Gelato ice cream cart in the summer.

Watkin Path Pools

ESSENTIAL KIT

In winter a pair of swim boots and gloves are essential as I suffer from Raynaud's. A woolly hat is a must. As a member of the Woolly Hatters Swim Group, it's a given!

SEA'S THE DAY

St Michael's Mount

21 CHALLENGES TO MAKE YOU EXTRA SWIM HAPPY

1. GOLDEN HOUR TO BLUE HOUR

See the sun dip over the horizon and then stick around for a little longer, for the magic blue hour of twilight. This is liminal time and space. As photographer Jannica Honey told us, 'It's as if the air becomes muddy or filled with something . . . it doesn't become clear any more. It's almost like the light itself touches your skin.' Do this on a tidal beach and really you couldn't get more liminal. You are at the edge of something, in between. Revel in it.

2. UNDER THE MOONLIGHT

There's not much that's more bewitching than a moonlit swim – whether it's a spontaneous dive in, under the moonbeams, or something planned and orchestrated. And a moonlit swim is well worth the planning.

Check moonrise times on a table or an app like Willy Weather. Look at the weather forecast – because you don't want to turn up for your glorious full moon, only to find it feels like the clouds turned the lights off. A full moon isn't entirely necessary – you can do it either side of full – so choose the best conditions for your moonbeam dip. Think, too, about where the moon rises and consider whether geographical features will impact on when it's first visible. It's best to choose somewhere familiar, whose waters you know well, so you have a sense of what is out there in the darkness. But be prepared to find it utterly altered. The moon will transform and enchant. Waterproof torches and lights are fun, but even better is revelling in the glow of that great big lamp in the sky.

3. SWIM SAFARI

Why swim in just one place when you can enjoy nature's playground in multiple spots on one trip? We have nicknamed this sort of adventure a swim safari, as it often includes a tick list of your ultimate swim location goals. Such days are sometimes defined by the number of swimsuit changes made – how about a three-cossie day? Just remember to clean or change everything between swims in different waters – be biosecure.

4. SKINNY DIP

What's more liberating than a starkers swim? Sometimes the water calls you unexpectedly. You stumble upon it, your cossie not to hand and there's no resisting. It seems the right thing to do, to throw clothes and inhibitions aside, jump in, submerge, with nothing between you and that water. There are other times when skinny is part of the plan. You do it with purpose. You have chosen your spot and know it's secluded, remote, far from the madding crowds. You're looking for whatever being naked in the water gives you – the feeling that you are free, wild, unashamed, rebellious.

If you can't bear the idea of the walk in or out, try taking off your cossie once you are in, then tie it around your wrist or waist, or put it on a rock as you swim and wriggle back into it before exiting the water. Have a towel nearby; you could bring a waterproof mat to put it on.

However, we recommend going the whole hog and embracing the potential awkwardness of walking in and out. Avid skinny dipper Jojo Clement says, 'I love being so closely connected to nature, the sensation of the water caressing my body is freeing and magical. Also I hate carrying soggy swimwear home. More people should try minimalistic swimming without the shame associated with being naked.'

5. SNORKEL SAFARI

Duck down into the sea, wearing a mask, and it feels like you've entered a dream world. There's nothing like having a window, as you swim, into the strange, wonderful life that lives and swims around our shorelines – sea squirts, crabs, sponges, starfish, anemones, the waving fronds of a kelp forest. Why not try the Sheringham snorkel trail, created by two divers in 2016, along the site of Victorian sewerage pipework off the Norfolk coast? See Katie Maggs's story (page 68) for more on snorkelling and wildlife watching.

6. CYCLE-SWIM SAFARI

A bike, a towel, a swimsuit – what more do you need? Relish the freedom of following a cycle trail and stopping off here and there for a quick dip. Pedal like mad and you'll warm yourself up in between, too. Try, for instance, Whitby to Scarborough, Llandudno to Prestatyn or even go for the whole fabulous big adventure of the Cornish Way.

7. FANCY DRESS SWIM

The fancy dress swim – it's impractical, ridiculous, downright silly: all the reasons that we love it. There's nothing like wading into the sea in some elaborate outfit that absolutely isn't meant to be there.

It's a sign of the joyous playfulness of the wild swimming community that there are so many people who share our love. Halloween, Christmas, Easter, birthdays ... so many great excuses to dress up! Check out @stivesmermaid and the hashtag formalfridaydipping for some fabulous ideas to add flavour to your swims!

8. SWIM PICNIC, SLOW STYLE

Summers are made for this. A dip in the river or sea, followed by a nice spread on the grass or beach, shared with others. We love, for instance, the idea of the Cambridge Slow Swim and Picnic – taking it easy and getting your priorities right!

9. SWIM IN THE RAIN

There's nothing more wonderful than being right in there and seeing the raindrops bouncing like diamonds off the water. You're going to get wet anyway, why not get doubly wet?

10. RUN-SWIM

Is there a better warm up after a swim than the run back home? You leave the water shivering, feet slide into trainers, numbed, and yet by the time you get back you're sweating and throwing off layers. It's absolutely exhilarating. The only question is how to perfect that neat kitbag for a run-swim change, or whether to do your pelt back still dripping?

11. GOING THE DISTANCE

Push yourself and sign up for a distance challenge. There are so many, so choose one, get training and, if you feel under-confident, book some sessions with a coach or join a club for motivation.

You don't have to put your name down for swimming the Channel or enter some hugely competitive race – challenging yourself can be about setting a distance target for your daily swims, swimming for a particular length of time, or simply building up to swimming to the buoy and back.

But if you are thinking of going big, here's a thought from inspirational speaker and former combat medic Simon Harmer: 'I've swum it twice now. The Lake Windermere swim is just really special. It has left an indelible mark; I think because it's such a big event. The first time I did it, I consciously wanted to ask the question throughout the 10.5 miles of the whole swim, *Could anybody do this, if they can swim?* And actually I think if you can swim two miles, or two kilometres even, then you probably could do Lake Windermere.'

12. DOGGY PADDLE

You and your dog in the water together! Heaven. What better swim buddy is there? And if you don't have your own canine friend, perhaps you can find someone who does. Make sure, though, that your dog is one that likes the water. You probably already know this from the enthusiasm with which they run in, but also you can check online what breeds are water lovers and enjoy a swim as much as you do.

13. GO FOR A PLIM

First there was plogging: jogging and litter-picking. Then came the plim: a swim combined with a pick-up of litter. Add a litter-picker, plastic bag and gloves to your kit, whether you're heading to a stream, waterfall, river or beach. Better still, set up or take part in a pick connected to Surfers

Kudhva, eco-retreat

Against Sewage, the Marine Conservation Society or your local Rivers Trust.

14. A WATERFALL POOL PLUNGE

Even better, follow a waterfall up through its plunge pools and try every one of them on the way. Waterfalls often feel like fun spots made for swimmers, but be careful to avoid them when they are in full spate, and if you are going to jump in, make sure to check thoroughly in the water for hazards beforehand.

15. PUT THE FUN INTO A FUNDRAISER

Why not do a swim challenge or organise an event in aid of a favourite charity or cause? One of our favourites is the fancy dress swim, but you can also do a dip-a-day or seize the challenge of a distance swim. On one memorable occasion we both swam dressed as Rosie the Riveter on International Women's Day in 2021 raising money for local women's charities.

River Dart

16. RIVER SWOOSH

Swooshing down a river with the current is one of the best experiences imaginable! Oh the joy of the riverbank, the feeling of floating along, or the hurtle of speed, watching the world go by from a duck's perspective. But you must approach with safety at the front and centre. Only attempt a swoosh with someone experienced and with all safety checks completed. Is the river in spate? Do you have a safe entry and exit point? How fast is the current?

It is all in the planning. It's definitely advisable to have someone drop you off at your entry point and then meet you with your warm gear at the exit. Another idea is to leave your kit safely at the exit point, run or walk to the start and then swoosh your way down again. This is only suggested if you are in a wetsuit or the water is a decent temperature.

17. KEEP A SWIM NATURE DIARY

Writing it down encourages you to observe so much more, to reflect on your swimming moods and the seasons, and to find things out. If you're wondering what the name of that gorgeous waterfowl is, or whether that seaweed is edible (yes, it probably is), you can go back and look it up, or even try a nature identification app.

18. HIKE-SWIM

Sometimes the joy of a swim is the getting there, the view on the way up the hill, the sweat it took. Sometimes it's the fact that you're miles from anywhere, save for a few other walkers. That kind of swim feels like a reward, the treat the landscape offers for those who venture further. Just be sure to plan well and take the right kit – the map, compass, waterproofs and head torch are as important as the cake. Your mountain skills must be up to scratch, it makes sense to go with pals who know what they're doing, and it goes without saying that you should take extra care when you're in the water – you are likely miles from help.

19. SWIM WITH A GUIDE

Go on, treat yourself. One of the best ways to be introduced to a new place and shown its swim-delights is to book yourself a guide. It's a lovely way to explore and can be great for newbies. Try, for instance, Les Peebles in the Yorkshire Dales.

20. RUCKRAFTING

The RuckRaft – a fully inflatable raft that can attach to a drybag or rucksack, created by Above Below – is so revolutionary, in terms of swim adventures, that it deserves a verb, *to RuckRaft*. Pioneering river trekker Fenwick Ridley told us how it transformed what he could do, allowing him to take all his stuff, and walk, scramble and trek the length of the North Tyne from Newcastle to Kielder. This simple piece of kit, which transforms any rucksack into a raft to tow across water, could expand your adventures too. You can go on a RuckRaft retreat, camp or guided swim, or make up your own trek and do it your way.

21. TRAIN AS AN OPEN WATER LIFEGUARD

Bonus points for this. Take on a challenge that could really make a difference by signing up to the three-day course delivered by the Royal Life Saving Society to earn your open water lifeguard qualification (OWL). You need no previous lifeguarding experience to do this.

To find a course, see rlss.org.uk.

In the UK and Ireland over 400 people on average per year accidentally die from drowning. Potentially your new skills could save a life.

Nanjizal

FINDING YOUR OWN PARADISE

RACHEL ANDREWS,
Southampton
Creator
▶ EVERYDAYATHLETERACH

I've always liked doing different and unexpected things. For me it's about the journey, the whole experience. It's about looking at the map and thinking about what might be there, and what it might look like when you get there, the kind of swim you might have. People tend to get so fixated on going to a particular place that it almost feels like location bingo, as if you've got to pick up a badge along the way. It has its appeal, but I don't really sign up for that kind of approach.

I'm more about finding somewhere that someone else hasn't been to. It might not be as beautiful as some of the other locations. But the beauty is in the peace and quiet, and having a place to yourself and feeling tiny in the environment. It's not often we get to feel completely insignificant in an environment and simply be an observer.

I travel around a lot for work and so I'm often staying at different places and looking for something to do. I always have my swimsuit in the car; it's just a matter of finding the right spot.

1 First, find some water on the map.
I tend to look for the nearest patch of water to where I'm going to be. I always tend to go for a river or the sea because lakes are so much more likely to be encased by private land, probably more likely to have fish and mites in, and, because of the static nature of the water, you're more obvious in a lake.

I like to seek out places where there will be either slow-moving water or, if it's quick-moving, there's no white water on it. I start off by looking at something like footpathmap.co.uk, which is useful because it (allegedly!) shows you all the footpaths in the UK. What I'm looking for is an-in-and-an-out, ideally a stretch of water where you've got a walkway all the way along, because then access is not controversial. I don't want to upset anyone, but equally, if the water is there I don't see why I can't get in it.

2 Study the water on Google Earth. Zoom in to see if it looks like the path is a line along which people do actually walk, or if it's some kind of farm track and you're going to stick out like a sore thumb strolling along, which wouldn't be good. I'll also study the water itself from the Google Earth perspective, trying to work out whether you can see white water on it or whether you can see reeds, which would mean that in summer that's going to be a bit more claggy but probably okay.

You should also keep an eye out for hazards like weirs – water that looks suddenly flat, or with structures around it, can suggest where there might be one. Also, is it just one colour? Then that's indicating, to me, that it's probably quite deep. And are there any wild changes in direction of the river? This might indicate a manmade structure or some disturbance. I'm checking to see whether there is anything that's going to upset the swim, although that might not put me off, because you can always get out before it.

3 Make sure to avoid fisheries or places where your swim might impact other users. Where I know there's a commercial fishery I won't go through unless it's the off-season, because those fishing folk are paying a grand a day to be there, and I don't want to put someone out who has spent that amount of money. I tend to think, 'Have that bit of water, I'll go to the beach or somewhere else.'

4 I like to act like I belong! I find if you do come across someone who thinks you shouldn't be there, it's best to greet them straight up. Use the charm offensive!

5 Look out for flashy rivers and waterfalls. Waterfalls can be great, adventurous dips, but the warning around them would be to look out for flashy rivers and have an understanding of what that looks like. Having seen one come up from ankle deep to thigh deep in a matter of minutes, I'm quite wary. I'll be looking at the colour of the water. If there's any mud, I'd be wondering why it's there.

6 Before I get in, I like to sight where I'm getting out. Sometimes that's not possible but mostly it is. Even if I can't see what's in between I'll have looked on Google to check, but knowing that my get-out is easy is important. Especially if you've got yourself colder than you

Lepe Beach

expected and therefore everything is so much harder work. If there's some kind of a manoeuvre or you've got to pull yourself out of the water, that can become a problem. I don't mind too much for getting in, but some kind of climbing or grappling with tree roots to pull yourself back out at the end of a swim – that's not ideal.

7 Wear something on your feet. When I swim in the sea, I'm mindful that I've got something on my feet so I can get out whenever I want to, and that the get-out is easy. It's so easy to terrify yourself. You don't want anything that makes the whole getting out process more difficult.

8 Check the tides and assess water levels. For a sea swim, the first thing I look at, if it's a new location, is the navionics app. One of its features is a sea chart which enables me to zoom in to see, without going to the beach, exactly what's going on with the water level.

At my local beach, Calshot, when the tide goes out, you've got a long walk before you can get in. It can be a real disappointment to turn up and then, especially on those long sloping beaches of the Essex coast, find yourself asking, *Where is the sea?* I want a metre and a half of water and I'll be really chipper with that – and that proviso will determine what time I go to the beach.

9 **Take a moment to check when you first get in what the sea is doing.** Whenever I get into the water, I always have a minute where I just bob about and get my breathing right. I'll look around and watch what's happening, comparing something close to me on the beach and something in the distance to see if they stay the same or if they are parting. That tells me how quickly I'm drifting. Then I always swim into the tide first, knowing that if I'm tired, I'll be able to drift back on the tide without any problems.

10 **Pack a tow float and tracker on your phone.** I have a changing robe and my car key and my mobile phone in my tow float. I take these no matter what. On my phone, I run a free app called RYA SafeTrx from which you can send a swim route plan, which it will text to your emergency contact. You set a time you're going to get out, then if you overrun, it will alert them, and if you are uncontactable, call the Coastguard.

11 **Be prepared not to go in.** If you get to the water and it's a non-event, then you probably had a nice walk getting there. You win some, you lose some!

WHY NOT CHECK OUT . . .

Lepe Beach
📍 **documents.shelved.grips**

In front of the lighthouse is a super location. You're at the mouth of the Beaulieu River, looking directly over at the Isle of Wight. There's always some movement of water in one way or the other, but you can swim there at any state of the tide – you just have to pay attention to what's going on with the water, and you need to stay beach side of the channel markers, because that's a channel where boats are coming in and out. It's always really interesting and super quiet. It's a short walk from the car park (pony.tradition.lightens).

It's an absolute haven, a Site of Special Scientific Interest, and you see flocks of birds coming up the Solent at sunrise. Once, as I was swimming back, I decided to swim on my back to see the sunrise, and when I turned around, there was a seal right next to me, big, like a massive Labrador. I have no idea how long it had been watching the sunrise with me. I've seen that seal a couple of times.

Lepe is really nice, it's wonderfully quiet. It's just you and nature, pretty much. And the weird thing about the Solent is you don't get waves – so you don't hear them crashing. It doesn't really make a noise. Most of the time it's like a moving lake.

THIS MAP IS FOR YOU TO DRAW

The art of wild swimming … it's not something we're pretending to have perfected. All of us are learning, finding our own way, through trial and error, and the tips and advice of the community around us. But in researching this book we feel we've tapped into the wild swimming hive mind and discovered new ways of doing things, new places to go, and a heightened awareness of what footprint we leave behind. There is, we found, not one art of wild swimming, but many, and we are all still collectively sketching it out.

One of the things we hope this book gives you is something similar to what it has given us – a map in our minds of England and Wales and their waters, that is marked not just by rivers, streams, waterfalls, lakes, reservoirs and bays, but by people. It is a map of swimmers as much as geography. It's a guide to a community that connects with the land. It's a list of places we want to go and swim groups we want to meet. We wish you fun, delight, adventure, wonder and surprise as you explore it. But we also want to inspire. Draw your own map. Create your own codes. Start your own campaigns. Protect your own local spots. Find your own new places.

Anna and Vicky

LOCATIONS, LOCATIONS, LOCATIONS

How did we source our locations?
The places in this book aren't all swim spots that we've visited. This isn't that kind of guide book – though some of the locations, of course, we have been to and know very well. Rather it's a guide that reflects the knowledge of a community. Swimmers contributed their entries, told us their local gems, and so we created together a map of the type we all wished we had. These swimmers are our gurus. We owe them huge thanks.

How are locations identified?
For each spot coordinates are given either for point of access or nearest car park. We chose to use what3words, which you can download as an app.

This is an easy way to describe any precise location. It works by dividing the world into 3-metre squares and giving each a unique identifier of three words.

It is used by emergency services, which means you can use the locations given in this book should you need to call them.

The three words are automatically generated; some of the combinations gave us a giggle!

Scan the QR code for access to the unique *The Art of Wild Swimming: England & Wales* Google Map. It shows you all the locations featured in this book, and you can use it to plan every aspect of your swim adventures.

ENGLAND

LONDON
Beckenham Place Park Lake 161
Bushes Outside Simon's House,
  Teddington Lock 161
Hampstead Ponds 10
Hampton 164
Love Open Water, London
  Royal Docks 160
Petersham Meadows,
  Richmond 165
Sunbury-on-Thames 164
Thames Ditton 165

THE MIDLANDS & EAST

EAST ANGLIA
Anderson's Meadow 142
The Cam, Upware 152
Ebridge Mill, North
  Walsham & Dilham Canal 136
Geldeston Locks Inn, Beccles 139
Grantchester Meadows 151
Hellesdon Mill, Norwich 137
Outney Meadow 138
River Deben, Waldringfield 141
Sea Palling 143
Shingle Street 141
Wainford Silo, Broome 139

THE MIDLANDS
Anchor Church, Milton 134
Boyne Water, Brown Clee 131
Carding Mill Valley Reservoir 130
Chatsworth 124
River Avon, Cleve Prior 148
River Avon, Marlcliff 147
River Soar, Mountsorrel 134
River Teme, Ludlow 132

Slippery Stones 126
Stoney Cove 135
Three Shires Head 125
Welford-on-Avon 149

THE NORTH

LAKE DISTRICT
Black Moss Pot, Borrowdale 49
Coniston and Peel Island 104
Coniston Water, Monk Park 102
Lake Windermere 10
Lake Windermere, Rayrigg
  Meadow 102
Rydal Water, south side 101
Wastwater 46

LANCASHIRE
Mary's Shell 106
Morecambe Bay 106

MANCHESTER
OpenSwim, Sale Water Park 128
Salford Watersports Centre 128
Uswim!, Salford Quays 128

THE NORTH EAST
Beadnell Beach 96
River North Tyne, Chollerford 95
Roker Beach 97
Seaham Slope Beach 98
Tynemouth Longsands 94

NORTHUMBERLAND
Coves Haven, Lindisfarne 7
Hethpool Linn 8
Sweethope Lough 93
Tyne Green 91

SOUTH CUMBRIA
Irish Sea, the Rocks,
  Hodbarrow 104
The Hollow, Hodbarrow
  Nature Reserve 105

YORKSHIRE
Broomhead Reservoir 121
Crookes Valley Park 121
Eel Pool, River Ribble 110
Gaddings Dam, Todmorden 118
Hardraw Force 112
Hayburn Wyke 8
North Bay, Scarborough 116
Ryburn Reservoir 115
Sandsend 109
Sparth Reservoir,
  Huddersfield 43
Stainforth Force 111
Waterswallows Quarry 123
Whitby Beach 108
Withens Clough 115

THE SOUTH

CORNWALL
Boat Cove, Pendeen 191
Cape Cornwall Tidal Pool 191
Housel Bay 188
Nanjizal Beach 187
Porthcothan 187
Porthtowan Tidal Pool 190
Prussia Cove 189
Trescore Islands 187

ISLE OF WIGHT
Freshwater Bay 194
Gurnard Bay 193
Osbourne Bay 194

SOUTHEAST
Andark Lake 175
Clifton Hampden Bridge 157
Cuckmere Haven 170
Heron Lake 175
Lepe Beach 241
Longbridges, Oxford 159

Marsh Lock, Henley-on-Thames	159
Ovingdean Beach	171
Shepperton Lake	172
Tankerton Beach	166
Walpole Tidal Pool, Margate	167

SOUTHWEST

Barricane Beach	181
Cheesewharf, Lechlade	154
Clevedon Marine Lake	177
Clevedon Pier	179
Cotswolds Country Park & Lake	10
Crazywell Pool	184
Farleigh & District Swimming Club	168
Foggintor Quarry	183
Lee Bay	181
Man o' War Bay	33
Neigh Bridge Country Park	153
Northam Burrows	181
River Avon, Batheaston	169
River Avon, Eastwood Farm	180
River Dart	54
River Plym, Cadover Bridge	185
Thames Path, Kemble	154
Warleigh Weir	168

WALES

NORTH WALES

ERYRI/SNOWDONIA

Criccieth Beach	225
Cwmorthin Quarry	219
Llyn Geirionydd	219
Llyn Idwal, Ogwen Valley	223
Llyn Llydaw	220
Watkin Path Pools, Afon Cwn Llan	224

SOUTH EAST WALES

BRECON BEACONS

Llyn y Fan Fawr	204

BRIDGEND

Merthyr Mawr	203

FOREST OF DEAN & WYE VALLEY

River Monnow, Skenfrith Castle	211
River Wye from Dixton Church to Monmouth Rowing Club	209
River Wye from Goodrich Castle to Kerne Bridge	210

SOUTH WEST WALES

SWANSEA

Blue Pool, near Broughton Bay	208
Bracelet Bay	208
Pwll Du	207
Rotherslade	204

THE GOWER PENINSULA

Langland Beach	200
Pobbles Beach	201
Port Eynon to Horton	200

CARMARTHENSHIRE

Broad Haven, Nolton Haven & Little Haven	216
Mwnt Beach	216
The Blue Lagoon	215

BOOKS YOU MIGHT ENJOY

Kerri Andrews, *Wanderers: A History of Women Walking*, Reaktion (2020)

Tamsin Calidas, *I Am An Island*, Doubleday (2020)

Lynne Cox, *Open Water Swimming Manual: An Expert's Survival Guide for Athletes and Open Water Swimmers*, Vintage (2013)

Anna Deacon and Vicky Allan, *Taking the Plunge: The Healing Power of Wild Swimming for Mind, Body & Soul*, Black & White Publishing (2019)

Roger Deakin, *Waterlog: A Swimmer's Journey Through Britain*, Chatto & Windus (1999)

Ruth Fitzmaurice, *I Found My Tribe*, Vintage (2018)

Tristan Gooley, *How to Read Water: Clues and patterns from puddles to the sea*, Sceptre (2017)

Kathleen Hart, *Devorgilla Days*, Two Roads (2021)

Alexandra Heminsley, *Leap In: A Woman, Some Waves, and the Will to Swim*, Windmill Books (2018)

Sarah Kennedy Norquoy, *Salt On My Skin*, Welford (2020)

Amy Liptrot, *The Outrun*, Canongate (2018)

Robert Macfarlane, *The Wild Places*, Granta (2008)

Joe Minihane, *Floating: A Life Regained*, Abrams Press (2017)

Adam Nicolson, *The Sea Is Not Made of Water: Life Between the Tides*, William Collins (2021)

Emma Jane O'Brien and Penny Wilkin, *Dips and Chips, the book: An Illustrated Guide to Where to Swim (And Eat) Around Central England*, independently published (2021)

Kate Rew, *Wild Swim*, Random House (2008)

Daniel Start, *Wild Swimming: 300 Hidden Dips in the Rivers, Lakes and Waterfalls of Great Britain*, Wild Things Publishing (2013)

Daniel Start, *Wild Guide* series to England and Wales, Wild Things Publishing

William Thomson, *The Book of Tides*, Quercus (2016)

Bonnie Tsui, *Why We Swim*, Rider (2021)

Victoria Whitworth, *Swimming With Seals*, Head of Zeus (2017)

IMAGE CREDITS

1, 64, 130-133, 196, 221 Beth Squire
2, 81, 250 Anna Moffat Photography
6 Vicky Allan
11 Goddard New Era/Alamy Stock Photo
15, 28, 31, 37, 226-231, 186-189, 236 Jo & Patrick Clement
20, 234 Roger Taylor Photography
23, 70, 233 Cat Vinton
25 Gavin Haskell/Alamy Stock Photo
27, 38-44, 120-122, 127 John Anderson
29 Salim Ahmed
32, 49, 108, 109 Ceri Oakes Photography
35, 68 Katie Maggs
36 William Thomson
45, 47, 57 Scott M Salt
48, 86, 160 Jonathan Cowie
50-51 Ella Foote
59, 90-93 Fenwick Ridley
61, 88, 100-103 James Kirby
75 Mark Brimacombe
79 Lizzie Patterson
94-95 Jane Barnacle
97-99 Becca Harvey
104-105 Jakki Moore
106-107 Serena Armstrong
108 Lucy Catherwood/Art Disco
110-111 Les Peebles

113 T.M.O.Travel/Alamy Stock Photo
114, 117 Ruth Craine/Alamy Stock Photo
115 Nicola Wilkinson/Ryan Wilkinson
118-119 Swim Feral
124-126 Tim Slater
128-129 Jade Hanley
134-135 Annie Brooks
136-137 Imogen Radford
138 Graham Turner/Alamy Stock Photo
140-141 Benellaswims
142 @swimspotsnorfolk
145 Loop Images Ltd/Alamy Stock Photo
146 Windmillskies/Alamy Stock Photo
147-148 Emma O'Brien
150-152 Clare Allen
153 Rebecca Ward
155 Anna Stowe Landscapes UK/Alamy Stock Photo
156-158 Katia Vastiau
162 Broni Lloyd-Edwards
162 Simon Turner/Alamy Stock Photo
164 Emma Richards
166 Dawn Steele
167 CBCK-Christine/Alamy Stock Photo

168-169 Sus Davey
170 Joe Minihane
171 Ian Goodrick/Alamy Stock Photo
172 Lorraine Candy
173 Shepperton Swim Lake
174-176 Simon Harmer
177-180 Rowan Clarke
181 Ruth Down
182 Craig Joiner Photography/Alamy Stock Photo
183-185 @devonswimgirls
190-191 Nicola Montfort
192 Simon Browitt/Alamy Stock Photo
193, 194-195 Madi Dew
193 Michelle Salsbury
198 Emma Lisa Jones/Alamy Stock Photo
199-201 Alison Owen/Alexandra Honey
202-205 Laura Truelove
206-207 Laura Minns
209, 210 Mark & Hayley Harvey
213 Amber Tipper
214-217 Tanya Knight
218-220 @cexx12
222-225 Tara Leanne Hall
238, 240 Rachel Andrews
242, social media and locations icons shutterstock

All other images by Anna Deacon.

The publisher and authors would like to thank all those who have generously contributed their photography to create this truly community-led book.